DATE DUE

Oct 24 03			
GAYLORD			PRINTED IN U.S A.

CRITICAL ESSAYS

CRITICAL ESSAYS

by

Osbert Burdett

Essay Index Reprint Series

BOOKS FOR LIBRARIES PRESS

FREEPORT, NEW YORK

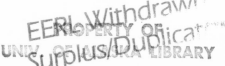

First Published 1925
Reprinted 1969

STANDARD BOOK NUMBER:
8369-1346-9

LIBRARY OF CONGRESS CATALOG CARD NUMBER:
79-99685

PRINTED IN THE UNITED STATES OF AMERICA

CONTENTS

PAGE

1. NATHANIEL HAWTHORNE 7

2. GEORGE MEREDITH 23

3. THE PASSION PLAY 44

4. JOHN GAY 66

5. PEACOCK THE EPICUREAN 78

6. TWO FOOT-NOTES ON PATMORE :
   I. Patmore and Divorce 104
   II. "A Daughter of Coventry Patmore (Sister
       Mary Christina)" 109

7. OSCAR BROWNING 114

8. THE POEMS OF ALICE MEYNELL . . . 122

9. SHELLEY THE DRAMATIST 135

10. THE ART OF MR. CHAPLIN 148

11. THE WRITINGS OF FRANK HARRIS . . . 156

12. VERS LIBRE 170

13. LITTERÆ HUMANIORES 177

14. THE AUTHOR'S TOOL 186

15. THE EFFECT OF PRINTING ON LITERATURE . 194

NATHANIEL HAWTHORNE

THE prose of Hawthorne is the most beautiful prose that has come out of America. Perhaps its fantastic quality of imagination, in which beauty kindles from word to word as colour will in tapestry or in the red glow against the dun background of a Yanina embroidery, picked out here and there with fragmentary touches of gold thread, is due to the fact that his sense of beauty was a changeling and had no father in American soil. His subject is the Puritan conscience, whose rigid quality was reflected in a stern law, the first refuge of frigid men who had entered a strange continent with all the forces of nature arrayed against them. Transplanted into a soil unprepared for them, the pioneers, who had revolted from their original home, identified their foes without with their foes within, so that nature everywhere became the enemy, and life itself sinful. To have been born at all was the first sin to these Puritans—who suffered from the most dreadful of all human superstitions, expiation by sacrifice. To them repentance meant living in sackcloth and ashes. But there is an old word not open to this confusion,

the word resipiscence.   It means, as repentance
should be held to mean, change to a better frame
of mind.   This they neglected.   The means
were confused with the end ; punishment was
enjoyed for its own sake, and duty became a man-
eating idol after the manner of Moloch.

What, then, could a sensitive and imaginative
descendant of these Puritans do but play around
the border of forbidden things, and seek satisfac-
tion in the perpetual, secret war between the
human spirit and the fetters which Puritanism
placed upon it ?   Since the human spirit was held
to be sinful, all the forces of life became forces of
evil ; and we watch in these novels one figure
after another in whom the spirit was not quenched
paying the penalty for its virility.   The mysterious horror is intensified because the victims share
the beliefs of their society, and are usually the first
to approve the judgments passed upon them.
These judgments, however essential to the frame-
work of the stories, often seem to us so monstrous
that we instinctively cry for a rebellious soul in
whom the evil spell which controls the conscience
of his neighbours has been broken, but we never
find him ; and the occasional relief which Hawthorne allows to them, as, for instance, in the cry
of Hester to Arthur Dimmesdale when they meet
in the forest : " What we did had a consecration
of its own.   We felt it so.   We said so to each
other.   Hast thou forgotten it ? "—this occasional relief becomes an added sin which intensifies

the victim's sense of guilt.   Yet Hester's words
are more convincing to us than Dimmesdale's
repentance for having momentarily accepted them,
so that we perceive Hawthorne's imagination to
have been instinctively right, and the judgment
which his upbringing accepted, an error.   In the
familiar case of the young wife married against her
will to an old and crusty scholar and deserted in a
strange land where she fell in love with the young
pastor, and was then exiled with her child from
the community in whose midst she had to live, we
should have thought that some one, in that Scrip-
tural society, would have remembered, if not
quoted, the famous words to the Magdalene's
accusers : " Let him that is without sin among you
be the first to cast a stone at her."   But no.   All
Hawthorne's hereditary conscience was implacable, except that inner instinct of his which enabled
him to present, but never without misgiving, the
forces of human vitality, the cry of the heart which
in such circumstances is the witness of religion
against morality.

All competent critics agree that Hawthorne's
symbolic power was alloyed with a tendency to
fanciful allegory, which, as Mr. Yeats has said of
rhetoric, is the will doing the work of the imagination.   The scarlet letter is repeated upon the
water in the wood, in the heavens at night, even
on the breast of another human being.   It is said
to be luminous in the dark or on the approach of
kindred evil.   But in *The Scarlet Letter* there is

one symbol which is never thus out-worn, never
allegorized, never explained, and that is the most
original of Hawthorne's creations, little Pearl,
Hester's daughter.   The only father of whom she
has ever been told is the Prince of the Air ; and
the elfish nature of the quaint child rejoices in the
mystery of her paternity.   She is masterly drawn,
and what does she symbolize ?   The secret link
between Hester and the Reverend Arthur Dimmesdale, Pearl is also the only human link between
her mother and the world.   She is the product of
the one original and sincere impulse that Hester
has known.   But since all original impulses are
evil to the Puritan and therefore excluded or re-
pressed, little Pearl assumes an elfish character, as
life is apt to do when prohibitions bar its free development. The vitality that is scouted asserts its freedom and mocks its mentors, rejoicing perversely
in all that isolates it from them, and remind-
ing them of the law, which they cherish, but from
which it is happy to be free.   Thus, from the
first Pearl is fascinated by the scarlet letter on her
mother's breast, and refuses to recognize her when
she has once flung it from her until she has again
replaced it there.

   Pearl is profoundly imagined.   She is life itself,
and offers, in mysterious and oblique ways, the
perpetual criticism of the spirit upon the letter, of
humanity upon its institutions, of imagination
upon reason, of life upon law.   The same instinct
was at work in the creation of Donatello, that

Pagan who bore something more subtle than any resemblance to the Faun of Praxiteles. Unlike Pearl, however, Donatello is drawn into the mesh of human society. He becomes less natural, more human ; we set the loss beside the gain and ask ourselves which is the greater. Contemplating the result in him, his fellow-victim (for Miriam and Donatello cannot be regarded as criminals in any but the most restricted sense), inquires :

" Was the crime—in which he and I were wedded—was it a blessing, in that strange disguise ? Was it a means of education, bringing a simple and imperfect nature to a point of feeling and intelligence which it could have reached under no other discipline ? . . . I dare not follow you, replied Kenyon, into the deep and unfathomable abysses whither you are tending.

" Yet there is pleasure in them. I delight to brood on the verge of this great mystery, returned she. The story of the fall of man. Is it not repeated in our romance of Monte Beni ? . . . Sin—which man chose instead of good—has been so beneficently handled by omniscience and omnipotence, that whereas our Dark Enemy sought to destroy us by it, it has really become an instrument most effective in the education of intellect and soul."

The Marble Faun, from which this passage is taken, was the last novel to be published in Hawthorne's lifetime, and contains there, perhaps, the final philosophy at which this charming centaur of poet and puritan arrived.　We say perhaps, for Hawthorne's art should not be intellectualized. A sense of the mystery of life is more important, at any rate to the artist, than any explanation ; but if one must catch the moon in a net, and put a bit in the jaws of a meteor, then we should say that this was the conclusion which he reached.　But conclusions with him were so shot with imagination, that we can hardly distinguish between the materials for his art and his own vision of things. The creation is atmosphere ; the mood is reverie. The Puritan conscience and the sense of sin were the two forces which most impressed him.　Over their reaction upon human impulses his imagination brooded.　Did he show any understanding outside that stern and narrow field ?

He did ; and in *The Marble Faun*, to which I must chiefly confine myself, we find the odd combination of Puritan intelligence and artistic imagination, sketched above, presenting us for once with his picture of the religious instinct.　The background is Rome, doubly rich in the ruins of Paganism and the Renaissance, through both of which the story winds its way with a leisurely, assimilative skill which I, for one, never find distracting.　There are but four principal characters : Miriam, with her air of mystery and " gloomy wrong," Kenyon, the young sculptor, Donatello, the Italian youth whose pedigree merges into mythology more ancient than his family's famous vines, and Hilda, the young American girl, who is an exquisite copyist of the old masters. She is evidently the Puritan ideal of womanhood, a Puritan saint, a type previously foreshadowed in the practical Phoebe of *The House of the Seven Gables*.

Hawthorne's genius never gave apter proof than in his choice of an occupation for Hilda. She could never convince us as an artist, being too circumscribed, cast in too narrow a mould, too thin in vitality. A copyist, on the other hand, in the imagination of most men, would have been feeble. But when Hawthorne's imagination touched anything directly it fused it ; and, just as we believe in the marvellous needlework and fantastic designs with which Hester clothed her little Pearl, and embroidered the scarlet letter, so we believe in Hilda's copies of old pictures. Her feminine and receptive imagination so gave itself to the pictures which attracted her that the process whereby they had been painted was reproduced in her own mind; and she, who could create nothing, could become for that very reason the brush in the hand of a dead master, the instrument of a greater intelligence, to which, with the rarest submission, she was ready completely to surrender herself. Turn to the early chapter wherein her gifts are described and her limitations justified and you will see what genius can make of limitation itself. This faculty of hers, so delicately portrayed, seems to me symbolic of her character. Her pictures were, however perfect, copies. She was a copy herself, her sanctity being a reflection of an imperfectly conceived ideal rather than its incarnation. For as a saint she woefully fails. Her refusal to take the hand of Miriam, her friend, after having been the witness of the latter's desperate remedy against her persecutor, is more odious to us than the act from which she shrinks. Her sanctity was so fragile as to be soiled by any contact with the world ! She was no friend of publicans and sinners. A hot-house plant, we cry, that has no native vitality or resistance ; a school-slate on which others have scribbled with no authentic superscription of her own. The secret of which she is the accidental possessor weighs upon her as heavily as the crime upon the luckless pair who under great provocation and in an agonized moment perpetrated it.

Through all the long summer Hilda is oppressed by her burden. The picture galleries where she was accustomed to wander increased her torpor ; and " for the first time in her life, Hilda now grew acquainted with that icy demon of weariness, who haunts great picture galleries. He is a plausible Mephistopheles, and possesses the magic that is the destruction of all other magic. He annihilates colour, warmth, and, more especially, sentiment and passion at a touch." It would be difficult to find in any other book—woven as this is out of the lives of artists and with its double background of ancient ruin and modern museum—an equally complete analysis of the effect of these galleries upon a lover of pictures when in an unreceptive

mood. Hilda grew " sadly critical, and condemned almost everything that she was wont to
admire." Her spirit became as chill as her feet
upon the cold floors, and left a " further portion
of vital warmth " in every room.

She is then drawn to the different churches, and
at last to St. Peter's, and the thirty-eighth and
thirty-ninth chapters give an astonishingly interesting description of the " world's Cathedral," of
which the very temperature is described, and also
of Catholicism. In so rich a procession of ideas
and of criticism one is at a loss to know where to
pause and what to quote. But there are two sentences which combine to show Hawthorne's appreciation of a religion not his own, and the lack of
resources which he found in his native Puritan
faith. " To do it justice," he remarks, " Catholicism is such a miracle of fitness for its own ends,
many of which might seem to be admirable ones,
that it is difficult to imagine it a contrivance of
mere man." Hilda went to St. Peter's not, this
time, as an artistic pilgrim, but, our New England
author remarks, to observe " how closely and com-
fortingly the Popish faith applied itself to all
human occasions," and to reflect that multitudes
would find no advantage in her own " formless
mode of worship." The infrequent periods of
prayer at the meeting house are contrasted with
the perpetual celebration of the Mass at one or
other of the many altars, and with the attendant
Saints, once men on earth, ever waiting to receive

individual petitions.   In the Cathedral the passing stream of people was perpetually interrupted
as one or another paused to pray, and their ready
access and disburdening are contrasted with the
pent-up remorse of those outside the church.
The chapels of the Virgin, however, repelled
Hilda, because she could find only earthly women,
perhaps the lover of the artist, in the pictures,
much as she longed for " a mother in heaven for
all motherless girls like herself."   At last she
came to the south transept, with its number of
confessionals, and exclaims, notwithstanding the
integrity of her Puritanism, " Can the faith in
which I was born and bred be perfect, if it leaves a
weak girl like me to wander, desolate, with this
great trouble crushing me down ? "   Passing by
the confessionals in turn with their inscriptions
" Pro Italica Lingua " and the like, she arrived at
one announcing the English tongue.   Obeying
an irresistible impulse, Hilda knelt and poured
out the story of the murder which she had witnessed, withholding only the names.   At her conclusion the priest stepped out and summoned her
to stand that he might speak with her face to face.
Her face, as she obeyed, had " the wonderful
beauty which we may often observe in those who
have recently gone through a great struggle and
won the peace that lies just on the other side.   We
see it in a new mother's face ; we see it in the
faces of the dead."   How beautiful is Hawthorne's observation !   The whole passage is knit

so closely that quotation is distressing, and we wonder whether to admire most the novelist's art in his description of the cathedral, or his insight into the human soul of this daughter of the Puritans, or his response to the appeal of the ordinances of a faith which neither he nor his heroine shared.

When I read and re-read this passage not long ago, because (if the reader will allow the confession) I had lately received the present of a torso thought to be a Roman copy of the Marble Faun of Praxiteles, I wondered if this passage were generally recognized to be masterly. It was therefore delightful to find the following in Henry James' charming book on Hawthorne in the English Men of Letters Series :—

" The purest touch of inspiration is the episode in which the poor girl deposits her burden. . . . If the book contained nothing else noteworthy but this admirable scene, and the pages describing the murder committed by Donatello under Miriam's eye, and the ecstatic wandering afterwards of the guilty couple through ' the blood-stained streets of Rome,' it would deserve to rank high among the imaginative productions of our day."

The above passage is also worth quoting as an extreme example of the strangely diverse appeals of Hawthorne's Italian novel. But Hawthorne's art would be dishonoured by any writer who sought more from it than the art itself. To burrow there for this or that passage agreeable to any group of readers would be like praising a waterfall

B

for its power to turn a mill.   But it is also true to
say that, if his art be single, yet his sympathies,
especially in *The Marble Faun*, have diverse claims
upon us.   It is so rich in different appeals that
our desire is, as it were, to number them upon our
fingers.

In *Our Old Home*, to advert to other neglected
riches, which describes the impressions left upon
him by his stay in England, Hawthorne gives,
among many others, a fascinating description of
the dark and stuffy coffee-rooms to be found in
many of our old inns.   The description is doubly
piquant to an Englishman because written by a
stranger born abroad.   He also records his criticism of Dr. Johnson : " He meddled only with
the surface of life and never cared to penetrate
further than to ploughshare depth ; his very sense
and sagacity were but a one-eyed clear-sighted-
ness.   But (he goes on, of Johnson's teaching) it
is wholesome food even now.   And then how
English.   The great *English* moralist . . Dr.
Johnson's morality was as English as a beef-steak."
That is a tonic criticism.   It reminds us who are
apt to assume sometimes regretfully that English
morality is final, how insular our morals are, how
circumscribed, how provincial.   What Englishman on occasion but, subconsciously perhaps, has
groaned beneath their weight, or felt the wearisome divorce between our professions and our
practice.   Would not the world be a honester
and happier place if our ideals were more con-

trolled and dictated by our practice, instead of our practice being so helplessly disguised by our ideals ? One wishes at least that the experiment could be tried for a season. It is, no doubt, the discrepancy between English pretension and English practice which has made Mr. Pecksniff recognized as the perfect Englishman abroad, which is behind the accusation of " a nation of shopkeepers," which explains the cry " perfidious Albion." The load is lifted by the stranger. He recalls us to the open air. Again, Hawthorne says in the same book, " Success makes an Englishman intolerable. . . . I shall never love England till she sues to us for help, and in the meantime, the fewer triumphs she obtains, the better for all parties. An Englishman in adversity is a very respectable character ; he does not lose his dignity, but merely comes to a proper conception of himself." How rarely does the Englishman read books which tell him such home-truths, and what refreshment a reflective person finds in them ! Do books on England by our many foreign visitors circulate only in their own countries ? I should be hard put to it to make a list even of American volumes.

The note-books are full of similar good things. The many trifles that they contain are said by Henry James to have been exercises in description, the description of simple things, because it is a great tax upon a writer's skill to make them interesting. This is a suggestive criticism, but

Hawthorne had a native sense of language, a
delicate touch peculiarly his own. He never
learnt to write. From the first almost he wrote
well, and the early *Twice Told Tales* include reflections on a town pump and the varied sights observed by a tall steeple. His style makes of such
thin themes as these acceptable and unaffected
writing. It is always a pleasure to read his prose.
It is less as if we read than listened. This gift is
such as to condone many defects. No one wrote
more beautiful openings to books. The stories
rise as shapely as a vase. But he could hardly ever
finish them. The form collapses, the story runs
astray, or loses itself, or peters out. There is,
again, a tinge of melodrama, inseparable perhaps
from the borderland of good and evil on which he
delighted to brood. Whether it be this, or
merely that the Puritan standard of judgment, in
which evil was made a dreadful preoccupation, is
dead in ourselves, I do not know, but it is certain
that the mysterious sin which shadows most of his
characters ceases to be convincing the moment its
secret is revealed ; and we learn to expect disappointment at the revelation. Hawthorne could
suggest everything, and the suggestion was to
himself more than the reality. Miriam's secret is
the more effective for being only half explained,
and the " Conclusion " which he added reluc-
tantly to *The Marble Faun* was a concession to the
cruder class of reader, for whom moreover it is
still not explicit enough. This postscript seems

to emphasize the unsatisfactory solution of the story. It does not mend, but marks the failure of the ending.

While the artist in Hawthorne recoiled from matter of fact solutions, since he aimed at atmospheric effect, there is a general consideration to be remembered. Every age makes a bogey of some crime. A hundred years ago it was the act for which Beatrice Cenci killed her father, of which Byron was accused, and for which Shelley's Laon and Cythna were condemned. The superstitious horror of this act had its artistic compensation. We now know that such recoils imply a morbid fascination. But to-day that superstitious horror is gone, and another bugbear has taken its place. Yet the change from superstitious horror to unexcited composure is as healthy as that which distinguishes the astronomer from the savage at the sight of an eclipse or a thunderstorm. But the change deprives us of an artistic effect. Of this Hawthorne was himself aware. Hence he lingered on the borderland of mystery and defined as little as he could, because he was more interested in states of mind than in their causes. The fine thing in Hawthorne, as Henry James remarked, was his interest in the deeper psychology ; and this explains why a book like *The Marble Faun* appeals not only to the critical and to the general reader, but also to the consciousness of particular groups. The artist enjoys the descriptions and the talk, except where Hawthorne remained obtuse

to the end, namely his strange misunderstanding
of the importance of the nude in sculpture.   In
the same pages the Puritan discovers a saint ; the
Roman Catholic an unexpected understanding, in
a hostile quarter, of the blessings peculiar to the
Church.   Here again the traveller finds a guide-
book to Rome and the untravelled an unrivalled
description of Italy.   The appeal of this book is
various though the artistic imagination which
fused all this should be our main concern.   It
was this which gave to us the wonderful portraits
of Hepzibah Pyncheon and Clifford—a pair that
so fine a story-teller as Mr. George Moore has said
would have enchanted Balzac—of little Pearl,
beside the many less good creations of the novels.
How remarkable it is too that an author with
Hawthorne's understanding of the human heart
should yet have never made the heart itself his
subject, and been content to brood instead upon a
dark corner of the conscience, in fact upon a dis-
ease !   Love is never a centre of interest with
him.   He deals only with its consequences.

But imagine, for a moment, his gifts concen-
trated on the centre of the circle, round the cir-
cumference of which his puritan imagination preferred to wander, and what a love-story he might,
if born and bred of European traditions, have
conceived !   This flight of fancy is not idle, for it
brings his gifts and limitations into a stronger
light.   As he was we are content.   Hawthorne is
a poet who has left us only novels.

GEORGE MEREDITH

ON February 12, 1828, George Meredith was born. During his long life this was virtually all the information known about him. No biographical reference contained more than this ; and who his father was, who his mother, where even he was born remained a mystery. The result of this personal reticence was that Meredith became a legendary figure. He was once supposed to be the natural son of some unnamed person of distinction, and rumour, quick to follow any trial, suggested Edward Bulwer, Lord Lytton, the novelist, for his father. The aristocratic legend of his origin was thereby sufficiently justified, and the attribution was plausible because the earlier novelist had adopted Owen Meredith for his pseudonym. Rumour was not authoritatively contradicted till Edward Clodd's " Recollections " appeared in the *Fortnightly Review* of July, 1909. For the biographical facts which follow, then, Edward Clodd is the authority.

Meredith's father was Augustus Urmston Meredith, a naval tailor of Portsmouth, at No. 73 High Street of which town George Meredith was born. His mother's name Mr. Clodd did not mention, but he quoted a saying of Meredith that " she was of Irish origin, handsome, refined, and witty." This was probably true, for Meredith surely owed to one or to both his parents the exquisite profile which Watts and Rossetti were to paint. The poet's grandfather was Melchisedec Meredith, the original of that famous portrait of a tailor, " the great Mel," in *Evan Harrington*. His mother, we are told, " died when he was in his fifth year, and the father, marrying again, emigrated to Cape Town where he carried on the business of a tailor for some years till his return, when he settled at Southsea." After leaving the somewhat obscure years of his infancy, we find that he was " practically left alone " till he was sent to Neuwied in Germany to complete a rather haphazard education. On his return in 1849 at the end of his nonage, he was articled to a London lawyer. A poet by preference, he soon abandoned the law, and till he could find free self-expression in literature, drifted, like many others, into journalism. He found work on provincial newspapers till, through his friendship with a former editor of the *Morning Post*, he was sent in 1866 to Italy as correspondent of that journal on the outbreak of war between Austria and Italy. It would be curious to see the dispatches that Meredith sent home, but it is to be hoped that no one will enable us to do so. All this time—" I wrote verse before I was nineteen" he told Mr. Clodd, and he was now thirty-eight—he had been writing without recognition, and so well, that many of his admirers insist that his first novel, *The Ordeal of Richard Feverel*, remains his best. It is highly characteristic, however, that before this appeared, in 1859, his earliest prose narrative was the fantastic Arabian entertainment of *The Shaving of Shagpat* ("written at Weybridge with duns at the door"). The very first of his published books was a volume of Poems. The date of its publication, 1851, has since become famous.

The dedication of these Poems to Thomas Love Peacock reminds us that Meredith had married one of Peacock's daughters in 1849. She was nine years older than her young husband and herself a widow. The marriage proved unhappy, and Mrs. Meredith's death in 1860 was not a matter for deep regret. Some five years later Meredith married again. His second wife was a lady with French blood in her veins, Miss Vulliamy. They lived happily together till she died in 1885. In the interval before his second marriage, in 1862 in fact, he joined Dante Gabriel Rossetti and Swinburne at 16 Cheyne Walk, Chelsea, in a famous, though transitory, arrangement. Still earning next to nothing from his novels and nothing from his poems, he became reader to the publishers Chapman and Hall. It was thus in an official capacity that Meredith became acquainted with the early work of Thomas Hardy, Samuel Butler and George Gissing. He

rejected the manuscript of *Erewhon*, "quite
wisely," as the author subsequently said : Meredith "reported that it was a philosophical work,
little likely to be popular with a large circle of
readers.   I hope (Butler continues) that if I had
been the reader, and the book had been sub-
mitted to myself, I should have advised them to
the same effect."   Just so.

The financial turning-point of Meredith's life
arrived at last with the publication of *Diana of the
Crossways* in 1885.   In spite of a pyrotechnic
introduction, the book gained great popularity.
There was supposed to be a topical basis for the
story, and this helped the public to swallow better
things.   By the success of this book Meredith
was able to retire soon afterward to Flint Cottage,
Boxhill, in Surrey.   There, in aristocratic seclu-
sion, visited by his chosen few, he spent the
remainder of his life.   During a quarter of a
century Boxhill gradually became the goal of many
pilgrimages, and the Surrey woods and Downs
which inspired much of his poetry have grown
identified with Meredith's name.   Boxhill is
now haunted, as Lechlade and Wessex and
Felpham are, by the imagination of the poet
which it had coloured.

There is no modern writer of Meredith's rank
whose personal history is more relevant to the
study of his imagination.   The mysterious atmosphere of romance that gave a legendary interest
to the poet during his life has not been dissipated

by the facts that I have summarized. His name still vaguely suggests an aristocratic writer, and this halo will serve him well when the inevitable reaction against his reputation, now triumphant, has subsided. The breath of legend distinguished him from most of his Victorian contemporaries who shunned legend as they might have shunned a beggar in the street. They did not know Who they were turning away. The most exuberant was Meredith, and he was congenitally free from this timidity. Therefore, as it were of right, destiny gave to this wonderful son of a wonderful tailor not only a romantic name, a beautiful face chosen by Rossetti for that of Christ in one of his pictures, but a fantastic origin together with an instinct to make the most, by mentioning the least, of his curious family connections. Everything conspired to give to the poet a fascinating and remarkable personality. The innocent mystery is worth recalling because all his great creations in fiction derived from his consciousness of it. The man was of the substance of his favourite dreams ; his dreams were a family portion, and his writings bear the authentic stamp of work at one with the life and the personality of their author. His origin and his life are in beautiful accord with the creations of his imagination. The lives of several of the Victorian poets, as I have remarked elsewhere, seem the reflection of their least beautiful poetry, and that the favourite poet of Queen Victoria should be a favourite poet of other poets leaves us ill at ease. We can never stifle our suspicion of those who seem to make the best of both worlds, for it is impossible to believe that there is no hidden discrepancy between these two contradictory standards of virtue.   The personality of Gladstone would give us even more of the creeps than it does at present if his writings retained the faintest claim upon men of letters.   It is with such men as Cobbet, Borrow, Peacock or Meredith that we feel perfectly open, because they make us feel that they have been perfectly open with us.   The men and their books can be recognized at a single glance.   The criterion that they invite is the same ; the taste of the two is identical.

Thus romance, the innocent habit of throwing gold-dust in the eyes of observers, is congenial to the character of a romantic personality, and Meredith's style raised a similar dust in the wake of his novels.   The novelist was primarily a poet, whose songs stammered themselves into sometimes beautiful verse and whose prose was so surcharged with the substance of poetry that language struggled and fretted with its weight.   Too much has been made of Meredith's difficulties, however. His obscurity has been exaggerated and his wit misconstrued.   Being an imaginative artist, he necessarily invented a new manner to express his view of the world.   The imagination can never rest content with familiar symbols, and it was his new symbolism, mistaken for an intellectual process, that puzzled his readers. Language is a highly developed medium for the intellect, which has no other means for communicating ideas ; but the imagination has invented as yet no final medium of its own. That is why it employs so many : that is the reason why there are so many arts, in all of which the imagination is equally at home, and why also the intellect is completely at home in only one of them, in literature. Because his readers have tried to apply to Meredith's style too intellectual a test, they have found difficulties. Meredith was a poet, consequently his prose is the prose of a poet, not that of an abstract thinker. All symbolism is obscure to anyone who is not sensitive to beauty : pictures, for example, are generally considered so obscure that even bad artists need to give descriptive titles to them. Meredith, again, thought more elliptically than most of his readers ; consequently his style, like Mallarmé's, reads as if sentences had been left out. He is impatient of conjunctions, and appears to go on thinking between the words. But to accuse him of exceptional obscurity is to exaggerate. He and Carlyle retained a love of the crusty German that they both had studied in their youth. The effect on both was to make them write English as if they were foreigners. They took a personal delight in the incongruous effect ; it was another proof of the plasticity of their native tongue. Such artistic jokes are natural to artists, and may come to be admired by their fellow-countrymen. We no longer find Meredith's prose difficult for we are now in the secret of his aim. The measure of a man's obscurity to his earliest readers may prove the measure of his interest to posterity. As a rule, only authors who have little originality can be read on their first appearance with absolute ease.

Let us see what the wit and the conversations which helped to make the novels of Meredith famous, will yield to our analysis to-day. Wit is known by a feeling of delightful shock, which is the result of the action of its two elements upon our perception. These two elements are gaiety of form and gravity of meaning. The presence, in perfection, of either element is often enough to occasion the use of the term. Since also there are many people with a happy turn for phrasing, the idea of wit tends to be confined to fun, and the strict example, which is by derivation philosophic wit, is less common. We may distinguish between the two by a simple test. The light epigram, unlike its greater fellow, will not bear stating in any other formula. Its only wisdom is its choice of words. Philosophic wit is rarely funny for its phrasing. Its centre of gravity does not lie upon its face.

The curious fact, however, about the wit of Meredith is that, while in kind philosophic, it received in England the tribute accorded to the ordinary epigram. This cannot be explained on the ground that his phrasing is relatively happy, because it is notorious that his language is lumbering, over-weighted, disdainful of Saxon brevity, and delights in long words of Latin roots.   Moreover, the antithesis or the play on words he rarely used. Meredith is the type of philosophic wit, but his cumbrous phraseology, such as " possession without obligation to the object possessed approaches felicity," is an odd basis for a sportive reputation. The remark growls, and if we smile it is because we know that the sage is meaning to be friendly. The truth is that Meredith was a born maker of aphorisms, and that these pass muster as wit with an unreflective people.   An aphorism has been defined as the concise statement of a principle, and to state a principle always seems funny to the English, who prefer to justify their actions rather than to act justly.   There is a wide difference, as they instinctively discern. We hardly know how to meet the statement of a principle except with silence or an awkward laugh.   The laugh seems to be expected when we meet with principles in a novel ; so the once famous " men may have passed Seraglio Point, they have not yet rounded Cape Turk," was quoted as a witticism !   Here Meredith was only finding a lame excuse for the employment of a metaphor.   It was lame because prose never came naturally to him.   But to see how the poet can command geography in verse, turn to the sonnet called " The Two Masks," where the exactly parallel metaphor of Cape Leucadia and

Mount Athos is used finely.   In sum, Meredith
was called a wit in England because he had an
aphoristic habit of mind, and in his prose the
latent poet was still able to attract attention to
his sayings by the artificial quality of his words.
The English could not conceive any moralist
dressing his novels with such dicta unless he was
trying to be funny, so, fearing to appear destitute
of humour themselves, they hailed him as a wit.
The wit of Meredith is the illusion of a wooden-
pated public.   He had matter in plenty, but his
manner was gnarled.

Being a man of immense vitality and imagination, he was a great humorist at heart.   The
wildest play of his humour belongs to an old
English tradition, indeed to a humanity that is
older than his race.   He had a rich store and was
capable of magnificent fooling, but Englishmen,
being instinctively aristocratic, and having learned
not to associate humour with plutocracy, could
not reconcile humour with a man of Meredith's
fine taste.   They expected wit of such a person ;
though, in truth, his gift for Comedy, of which
he was a connoisseur, was less developed, in his
characteristic creations, than his instinct for the
extravagantly comic.

So with Meredith's conversations.   A friend
of mine who admired Meredith's novels once
remarked : " If any woman dared to talk as
Diana does, she would be thrown out of the
window."   That is true.   Not even the conver-

sation that is written for the stage much resembles private talk. It is too logical and coherent in form. Henry James achieved a close reproduction of ordinary converse in his novels, but the result was that no one at first could follow its drift. Its apparent subtility was partly caused by the inconsequence that it copied from ordinary talk. The method of Meredith is different. As it was by the scattering of aphorisms in his descriptions that Meredith achieved the illusion of wit, so it was by exchanges of repartee that he produced the illusion of conversation. In *The Tragic Comedians* there is a characteristic example. Soon after the book opens, the aristocratic Clotilde contrives to attend a public function at which the notorious democrat, Alvan, is to be present. She has romanced about him wildly, and, reckless of all but admiration for the personality that captivates her on report, she attends to experience for herself the gulf that separates her hero from ordinary mortals. He towers there, as her imagination had pictured him, a king among men. The young woman approaches the select group which surrounds him, and with a fiery word breaks into their conversation. The vivacity of her remark saves her ; she is led away by her hero to a corner, where in a kind of dream she hears him talk. The great man warms to his subject, expatiates, overwhelms. At the end of an outburst to be counted in paragraphs, he breaks off as follows :

You leave it to me to talk.
Could I do better ?
You listen sweetly.
It is because I like to hear.
You have the pearly little ear of a shell on the sand.
With the great sea sounding near it !

The illusion is charming, but it depends upon a fine disdain for verisimilitude. Only the opening exchange preserves any resemblance to speech. The four following cadences are wholly literary : the words not speech but writing. The effect depends upon an art that has expelled Nature so completely that, at such a moment, we would not have her back on any terms. In so far as the passage seems profound, it is because its substance is poetical. Can we conceive it to be uttered successfully upon the stage ?

Turn to any of the world's remarks that are witty for their matter only : " It is not so difficult to believe in God provided one does not define Him " ; or the words put by Flaubert into the mouth of Apollonius of Tyana as a last taunt against St. Anthony : " Let us leave him. He believes like a brute in the reality of things." These are pithy sayings, but a conversation conducted entirely on their level would shortly end in blows. Yet it was by adopting this form for his model that Meredith achieved the illusion of witty conversation. Its very disregard of verisimilitude gives a certain delight. His style was curiously uniform : even when his matter was

slender he was able to seem a fountain of intellectual activity.   We are not denying the feat
when we distinguish its qualities.   Meredith was
a great improviser with words.

His manner did not desert him in his poetry.
What of the poet who lay beneath ?

George Meredith will one day be recognized
as the least rustic and most intellectual nature-
poet we have.   His sensations were largely ideas,
and he sang of nature and of " brain " with equal
ardour.   To him intelligence was one of civilized
man's instincts, and the unnatural thing to him in
human nature was a fool.   His nerves seem to
have been composed of grey matter, and without
being an exceptionally profound thinker, there
was at least no cell in his body that did not think.
His state of mind, incandescent with intelligence,
is fixed in one of his last and shortest pieces ; it
is typical of the current with which the whole man
was charged :

> Open horizons round,
> O mounting mind, to scenes unsung,
> Wherein shall walk a lusty time :
> Our earth is young ;
> Of measure without bound ;
> Infinite are the heights to climb,
> The depths to sound.

Meredith's mind was always mounting, and alive
to the possibilities that lie for man ahead : above,
if he will climb them ; back to the time when

" mind was mud " if he will not. The certain
risks, the possible reward, made the romance of
existence. Meredith was a curious figure in his
generation because he was a great romantic
who was not a Christian. " I have never swal-
lowed the Christian fable," he said. The main
source of modern romance being thus denied to
him, Meredith fed his romantic imagination on a
theory of Nature which accepted her as a kind of
fairy godmother. She was a real mother, but she
promised wonderful gifts on condition that certain
simple but apparently pedantic rules were obeyed.
If we were " to wing our green to wed our blue,"
we must humbly and sensibly study the conditions
that made flight possible. The laws of the spiritual world, like those of the natural world, must
be obeyed to the letter if we were to gain advantage over them. A sense of humour was to
rescue the fallen Icarus from despair at learning
that waxen wings were not what Nature asked
of successful airmen. Even for us " to foot at
peace " with Nature she must be first obeyed.
Once we accepted obedience, and applied brain
to learning how to obey correctly, our reward was a
whole, new, enchanted world. This exalted common sense is the kernel of Meredith's philosophical poetry. A sentimentalist to Meredith was a
man who refused to think, a man content to stick
in the mire of idealism, emotion, lack of ideas.
This eternal fool is the eternal butt both of Nature
and vigilant comedy. Indeed Nature herself,

with her ineluctable laws, is the ultimate source of the Comic spirit. Brain is the study and worship of this nature, and is necessary to redeem man from the unnatural state of folly.

This interesting and unexpected identification of Nature with Intelligence enabled Meredith to write philosophical poetry on natural themes, and to compose lyrics warm with emotion in praise of intelligence. He wrote of Brain as if she were a mistress, and of Nature as if she were an idea. We find ardent love-poetry where we expect to find philosophy, and metaphysical counsels where we expect lyric description. When he writes of Earth, either Brain or Nature may be intended. His originality as a nature-poet resides in this identification of the two.

He once said to Clodd : " Chiefly by that which emphasizes the unity of life, the soul that breathes through the universe, do I wish to be remembered. . . . It is my verse for which I care most." Meredith therefore was as much the poet of Mayfair as of Westermain, for he declared that " earth's secret " is read only by those

> Close-interthreading Nature with our kind.

Thus, no other poet of Nature was so much at home in drawing-rooms, and no other master of comedy was more in love with the west wind. The spirit of Pan in nature, and the spirit of comedy in society, were the two guides of mankind, and they were closely knit in Meredith's philosophy because each also served to correct the excesses of the other.   A due balance of both in ourselves constituted the sanity which he was never weary of recommending.   To fire this conception with imagination is the aim of the poems, but they need mental alertness in their readers.   This, but only this, solves their frequent verbal difficulties.   The temptation of Meredith was to be content with a tissue of highly condensed images, and to regard the product as communicable poetry and perspicuous thought. The connections have to be supplied by the reader.   To do this, a sympathetic mood is required, and few people capable of enjoying Meredith's poetry always command it.

If Meredith identified Nature and Intelligence in his poetry, it was inevitable that he should do so in his novels.   Being also the poet of intelligence in men and women, he became the poet of an ideal aristocracy, as William Morris was of an ideal peasant state.   " There was fun in Bagdad," with which he began.   There was wit at Versailles, in the English equivalent of which he ended.   Meredith is one of the few writers who could be master of both, and find in the two the tonic touch of ridicule.   But for the most part he was concerned with the manners, the ideas, the intellectual atmosphere certainly, of a highly civilized leisured class, and he can distil exquisitely its beauty and distinction.   One could tell, without reading his modest paragraph in *Who's*

Who, that he was "a great reader of French"!
One could tell that he had wandered in the gardens of their châteaux. He is the poet of Versailles, the Watteau of English letters. The subtlest of the arts is comedy, and it exists in perfection in an aristocracy or nowhere. Every other class has some one above it, every other class is anxious to rise. This destroys the possibility of good manners, of which comedy is the artistic flower. An aristocracy can do easily what everyone else is trying to do, and the absence of struggle gives to its members the repose that is impossible to all below. The comedy of manners is its delight because it is the only class with enough leisure to study motives and characters. In extravagant fun, in the fine shades of comedy, Meredith was happy and at home, but the moment he left these extremes of life he found himself in difficulties.

All acute readers of Meredith must have felt a dualism present in his work. The explanation of his weakness depends upon an understanding of it. *Harry Richmond* is one of the most delightful of his stories, but we find a hint in that book with its less exclusive outlook that the author's mind is troubled. The canons of aristocracy are trampled under foot in a world invaded by industrialism. Feeling this, and being a man of genius, Meredith felt impelled to confront the contradiction. Telling a story, writing a novel, is not the only way of presenting life for an intelligent man. The world of ideas as well as the world of men offers a universal field, though the two are never independent. Meredith therefore turned to the ideas that were stirring the Europe of his day, and we find *The Tragic Comedians* and *Beauchamp's Career* with Alvan the democrat and Dr. Shrapnel the radical. It is fascinating to watch Meredith engaged with social theory in the second book. On the one hand there is the bias of tradition with its immense æsthetic appeal to him ; on the other there is the struggle of the man of genius to admit the new ideas that are hostile to the remnant of that tradition. Inevitably he wavered. All his instinct is for Mr. Romfrey, all his acquired argument with Dr. Shrapnel. Indeed so far does reason beguile him after the radical doctor that he feels he must atone. This is the reason why Dr. Shrapnel is thrashed by Mr. Romfrey. Meredith, as much a slave to plot as the incorrigible Dickens, has the English love of ending argument by force. Something vital was at stake, but it is amusing to find the knock-down blow in the most intellectual of English novelists. It is fair to remember that the order which he loved was passing as he wrote. His centre of sympathy was in the eighteenth century, and, though he did not pretend to be writing always of his contemporaries, he thought of his own day as feudal still. A sense of confusion at the dreadful change pervades many of his books, and there was somewhere in him a queer vein of puritanism which, as always, demanded sacrifices.

Has anybody read *Richard Feverel* and doubted this ? For the first three-quarters of the story this does not appear, but the moment Richard and Lucy are married something mysteriously happens. We are asked to believe that it lies in the characters of the lovers. But are they there to be changed ? A new novel seems to begin with new people. They have been sacrificed to something external to themselves. It is not the tragedy from which one revolts, but the improbability of it. In most of his long novels he tired before the end, and few are free from one priggish masculine character.

The women of Meredith are rarely afflicted with self-righteousness ; his men are. His deepest intuitions were of exuberant, free spirits such as Richmond Roy ; but, perhaps half-afraid of them, he also created a type of earnest-minded young men like Redworth in *Diana of the Cross-ways*. These men are prigs and represent the tax paid by Meredith's genius to the vulgar conception of good taste. He could not have believed in these gentlemen because none of them is convincing, not even Matey Weyburn, the least priggish of all. His great feminine creations are the Countess de Soldar and Emilia, while even Laetetia Dale is not so hidebound by conventional notions of duty as Redworth or Wilfrid. Why was he more often in a state of grace when he was writing of women ?   The answer may be that woman is the one natural thing tolerated by an aristocratic society.   Who so well can expose the follies of men as a witty woman, who discern their weaknesses so fast ?   Indeed the attraction of cultivated men and women for each other is largely in their respective power of exposing each other's shortcomings.   A sense of comedy gives a keen delight even to the victims of its exposure, and the opportunities for experiencing this delight is the best of aristocratic privileges.   It was really in the hope of enlarging the play of comedy that Meredith became a champion of the women.   It was her possession of the comic spirit that made Florence Nightingale so formidable, and many sisters walk in dread of their brothers from the same cause.   Comedy is a civilizing agent, and as the flower of urbanity is aristocratic, comedy, the aristocratic art which spares nothing at all, can be recommended universally.

Meredith's essay on Comedy is the finest in English, and with his charming dramatic frag- ment, called " The Sentimentalists," one cannot but regret that the English stage of his day gave no opportunity to Meredith's genius.   His novels were a series of situations, and alike in poetry and prose, he dramatized whatever he touched.   Two particular achievements remain to be recorded. He is the one English novelist who has created in Renée a Frenchwoman acceptable to France, and he is, I think, unrivalled in his capacity to express the romance of first love both in prose and in poetry. " Love in the Valley " and " A Diversion Played upon a Penny Whistle " are the very rhapsody of romantic youth, and the later song, " Ask, is love divine ? " finds romance in the experience that brings to most men disillusion and regret.

THE PASSION PLAY

THOUGH many books and articles have been written round every decennial performance of the Passion Play at Ober-Ammergau, and the drama has so many points of deep interest that it requires altogether exceptional control in any writer who sees it not to record his impressions, I think that there is still something to be said. With the conviction that the play could not be performed in any other theatre or by any other actors, abides the assurance that its chief virtues, its atmosphere of uniqueness, can yet be shared by the majority necessarily unable to make the pilgrimage. If I can persuade the reader to this paradoxical conclusion, perhaps I shall have deserved my own good fortune. Let me, then, try to show him the simple means whereby he can make a spectator's experience his own. It is doubtful if *The Ring* can be enjoyed thoroughly anywhere but at Munich or at Bayreuth. It is certain that, in England, Shakespeare is himself only at the Old Vic. Ibsen demands to be played in cycles. But the Passion Play, which could not be transplanted, can be experienced in the study by any-

one who studies its traditions, its history, and
(above all) its text, with the aid of the magnificent
sets of photographs that are available.   Of course,
some intimate effects will be lost.   The music,
which has never been published, will be wanting.
The peculiar virtue of an open-air theatre, to
realize which the Greek model at Bradfield should
be visited, remains to seek.   But, notwithstanding every qualification, the Passion Play is at least
as much at the beck of every English stay-at-home
as are the plays of Shakespeare to a reader who has
no other resources but his own imagination, a
pocket volume, and a restful day or two in bed.
The kernel of the Passion Play is in the words.

    The evidence for this is clear.   The play is in-
tensely dramatic, and its dramatic appeal is over-
whelmingly enforced by its religious end and
meaning.   Ritual was born at the birth of religion, and tragedy arose from the religious dance.
Consequently, a religious tragedy, cradled in tradition, and itself a rite growing from and belong-
ing to the living Christian faith, has every human
resource at its disposal.   The faith is in our bones.
It runs through the veins of those who most fierce-
ly oppose it.   Indeed, they are often tortured by
an unrecognized instinct from which they cannot
escape, as the poor are by an unrecognized claim
to property.   Even were it artlessly presented,
our instincts would make us prepared spectators
of the Passion Play.   But, besides this, directly
or indirectly, all the arts are laid under contribu-

tion ; and you have only to ask yourself what your images of Jerusalem and the Apostles would be, if no pictures had ever been painted, or statues carved, or reliefs designed, to realize that your mental pictures of religious history are not yours at all.   They are only an inheritance, a fief of the imagination in which, by the magic of art, the Christian memory has been enshrined.   The five senses are five roads, and for seven hundred years every one of these roads has been dug, fortified, and adorned by the Muses to direct you to the Holy City.   There are no other roads, no other road-makers.   This particular way has been pre-pared by Art, and prepared at the dictates of Christianity.   One of the lessons taught by the play at Ober-Ammergau is the incalculable part played by the arts in giving outline and definition to the Christian consciousness.

But, till you visit Ober-Ammergau, these mental pictures remain like a group of tesserae scattered about the mind, as in a confused jumble of broken mosaic.   You have never seen them all, at once, in their order, and place and relation.   The pattern has never been completed, nor the design properly pieced.   It is, then, with a strange flash of recognition that they suddenly align them-selves upon the stage.   You are the target for a hundred arrows that, for years whistling round your head and by your feet, suddenly all focus themselves upon your heart, co-ordinate its memories and define their form.   Well, if the play produces this intense effect on the spectator, is it not obvious that an effect more intense than he has felt before can also move the reader of the text and the student of the photographs ? For the reasons given above, the effect of the words and illustrations is more powerful than the sight of any less traditional drama. Its occasion, and the rich imaginative material upon which it works, are alike unique, for Ober-Ammergau has, also, its monopoly. To make the effect yours, let us turn first to the village and the theatre.

While the crowded train climbs from Munich at almost walking pace into the Bavarian highlands, you recall how in 1633 the inhabitants of the village vowed to present the Passion every year if the plague from which they were suffering should be stayed. Their prayer was granted, but, as if to remind them that such vows are not lightly to be taken, the representation has often been threatened, and has only endured to this day in spite of many attempts to suppress it. These attacks were nearly successful at the beginning of the nineteenth century, and might not have been foiled had there not appeared simultaneously three men of remarkable ability in the village. A convenient account of them is given in Mr. Hermitage Day's little book. Ottmar Weiss (1773–1843), a monk of Ettal, substituted for the old rhymed version a prose text closely following the Gospels. He also introduced the tableaux, and thus overcame many objections pressed in 1810. His

pupils were Daisenberger and Dedler.   The one,
Rochus Dedler, the village schoolmaster, composed, in 1814, the music for the chorus.   The
other, Daisenberger, the parish priest, remodelled
the text.   This was an immense task, and is so
well done as to deserve careful study.   The result
of their united efforts was to save the play from the
general suppression of such representations enforced at this period by the Bavarian Government.
The Prologues were added by the priest to intro-
duce each tableau, of symbolic significance from
the Old Testament, before each scene of the drama.
Before the curtain rises on these tableaux, the
chorus enters, explains the purport of the scene,
and, withdrawing to form an arc on either side of
the tableau-picture, sings a song descriptive of the
event portrayed behind them   As in the Greek
drama, the chorus is the ideal spectator, and the
music which accompanies its singing is designed
to express the emotion that the spectators are intended to feel from what they see.

   But we shall only confuse ourselves until we see
the space and disposition of the stage that make
these effects possible.

   The Opera House in Paris has a huge stage ; it
is the largest theatre in the world, according to
Baedeker.   The front row of its stalls contains
twenty-four chairs on either side of a central gang-
way.   Supposing that two chairs be placed in this,
you would have a stage at least as wide as a com-
fortably spaced, but concave, row of fifty people.

The Covent Garden stage has, perhaps, a similar width.   But both are dwarfed to insignificance by the stage at Ober-Ammergau.   Though the rows of seats are straight, not curved, and the *stage* is set in the open air, it is not dwarfed by the crests of the mountains seen above it.   Your first sensation is that the stage is as wide as the outside length of Olympia.   In each row there are a hundred seats, or twice as many as at the Opera House in Paris.

Every effect, then, depends upon the use to which this mighty space is put.   Between the front row of the seats and what we call the foot-lights, though this theatre receives all its light from the open skies, is the orchestra.   Above their heads appears the floor of the stage, which then recedes without any interruption for a considerable distance, until, in the centre, the front of a Greek theatre rises from it.   This theatre occupies only the centre of the vast stage.   On either side of the theatre, as in front, is a wide space.   The Greek theatre is thus isolated.   The space on each side of it is a street.   The space in front of it is used as a street.   But beyond either side street is a house, led up to from the main stage by a flight of steps.   Thus, looking at the whole stage from left to right, the spectator sees, in turn, a house, a street, a Greek theatre, another street, and another house.   The house on the left is the home of Pontius Pilate.   The house on the right is the house of Annas.   To traverse the whole the eye

D

has to travel from side to side as when it views a panorama.

Even were a photograph available, these details must have been insisted on, because some of the fine effects of the play depend upon them. The design is also interesting because it displays the advantages of the Elizabethan stage. The stage within a stage was of the first importance to Eliza-bethan drama. That the inner stage here looks like a complete Greek theatre, not only evokes our sense of tradition, but also suggests the city as Pilate might have known it in his own time.

Since these features are structural, and cannot be changed throughout the play, to bring them before the eyes is to go to the Jerusalem of the drama. In this setting, too, the effects that can be gained from a crowd of 700 persons, the number which takes part, can easily be imagined.

The present theatre, which seats about 4,000, was opened in 1900, and the auditorium (smaller but not unlike the inside of St. Pancras Station) is as simple as the stage is splendid. The seats are of wood, but cushions can be hired for three marks. Such details, I think, bring the visitor's sensations before us, and show that it is in despite, rather than for the sake of, cosmopolitan tourists that the play has become famous. Its object is edification, and few or no concessions, except the cushions and the roof, temper the rigour of attention. For example, the theatre, at this altitude, is extremely cold, and to sit the play through is impossible

without thick coats and rugs. The drama starts
at eight and continues till twelve. After an
interval of an hour and a half, the second part
begins. It continues till six. The actors are
permitted no wigs or make-up, and can therefore
be recognized in the streets by their long hair as
they serve in shops, drive cabs, carry luggage, or
pursue their natural occupations. The play was
originally performed in the churchyard, and its
present form, apart from the existing theatre, may
be said to be about fifty years old. Mr. Day says
that the present text was used for the first time in
1850. There has been growth, but no change.
The drama has been kept alive, not by novelty,
but by an ever deeper devotion to tradition. It
was, I think, in 1870 that the performances were
made decennial. The preparation for them, and
about half the population of the village directly
takes part, makes (during the year of representation) almost all other work impossible. Yet in
ordinary times this, like other agricultural villages,
is practically self-supporting. Consequently the
interruption of a whole year, beside a previous year
of preparation, is very serious. This fact partly
explains several attempts to suppress the performance. Those who embrace the economic inter-
pretation of history can be made a present of this
point !

In the interests of truth it should be added that
the revisions made by Daisenberger suppressed
the devils and the comic characters, without whom

no mediæval Mystery play was complete.   Indeed
they encroached so much upon the *Miracle* plays
that they brought them into disrepute, and led the
Church to withdraw her patronage.   This helps
to explain the secular character of Shakespearean
drama, and the origin of the hatred of the stage
that actuated the Puritans under Elizabeth, and
has continued ever since.   An attentive reader of
the Passion Play will realize, even from the present
text, that Simon of Cyrene was originally a comic
character, and his momentary reluctance, when the
soldiers enrol him to carry the Cross, suggests how
this incident must originally have been expanded.

The most notable achievement of the play itself
is to show the incidents of the story as they
appeared to the protagonists at the time.   By
virtue of the text, the clock is put back nineteen
hundred years, and, in consequence, the heroes
seem to be, as they seemed to the eyes of contemporaries, not our Lord and His disciples, but
Annas and Caiaphas, Pontius Pilate, and Dathan,
a trader.   The world apparently triumphed, and
we see every event through the eyes of the authorities.   Dramatically, too, all the disciples are
dwarfed by the figure of Judas ; and his conduct is
represented to have been, as in everyday life we
constantly discover, not the outcome of an evil
will, acting with deliberate malice, but the fruit of
a disintegrating conscience, gradually, and indeed
unintentionally, producing a tragedy so appalling
that he could never have planned it himself.   He

drifted to disaster, as you or I might do. A
stronger man would have avoided participation in
his victim's ruin. Judas was weak ; his character of poor rather than wicked material ; and
when he realized what he had done, he crowned
his weakness by committing suicide. The agony
of Judas is the counterpart of the Agony in the
Garden ; and their juxtaposition heightens to the
last degree the effect of both. The Potter's Field
becomes a place of pity and terror : the Garden of
Gethsemane a place of which one cannot speak.
Priest and dramatist in one, Weiss and Daisenberger in their text show a grip of human character that many, of either calling, might envy.

The singular understanding of human nature
that presents us with the Judas of the play, with
equal effect develops, from the pregnant hints in
the Gospels, the characters of Pontius Pilate,
Annas, and Caiaphas, and the rest. We stand in
their shoes, and cannot escape the question :
Would you not have acted as they did ? How
they came so to act is unfolded from moment to
moment till the end. There are, in all, seventeen
acts. Seven in Part I and ten in Part II. It is
an epic drama, a " history."

The first division is from the entry of Jesus into
Jerusalem until His arrest in the Garden of Gethsemane.

Since the general impressions that I have
read failed to convey the cumulative effect of the
procession of events, which is the essence of the

drama, I will try the reader's patience while, adopting a humbler method, I follow the opening of the
pageant on the stage.   After that, a touch here and
there upon its more suggestive moments should
suffice to make him read the play in full at his leisure.

You wait before the empty stage.   Then, as the
chorus files in from either side and sings the pre-
lude, nineteen hundred years recede, as you next
witness, on the inner or Greek stage, the first
tableau :   the Fall.   When the accompanying
song is over and the chorus has withdrawn, you
hear, in the distance, the noise of a joyful multitude.   Down the street by Pilate's house, upon
your left, there appears the head of a long procession which fills the road and winds across the stage
in front of the inner or Greek theatre.   Men,
women and children, some bearing palms in their
hands, and spreading garments on the ground,
pass in happy disorder till in the rear is seen our
Lord riding upon an ass.   He blesses those who
throng round Him.   He dismounts and advances
towards the Temple, which the inner stage now
reveals.   There the money-changers and the dove-
sellers, with their cages beside them, are driving a
busy trade among another throng.   His presence
commands a sudden silence, and He addresses to
them the familiar words.   The priests, not understanding the interruption, stare at the intruder,
and when they ask who He is, are startled by the
shout of the multitude :   " It is the great Prophet
from Nazareth in Galilee ! "   Angered at this

demonstration, the priests attempt to remonstrate. But, disregarding them, He overturns the tables so that the money rolls upon the ground. Then He overturns a cage of doves, who fly upward, out of sight, into the sky.

The vision of their flight is a cherished memory with every one. It is also a portent of the terrible realism that is to follow.

The traders' cries of dismay and appeals for compensation have hardly had time to make themselves heard when He seizes a rope, hanging near at hand, and twisting it round His hand drives them before Him. You feel—and how the feeling gives the scene its historic air—that, had they not been taken completely by surprise, they would have offered some resistance. The attitude of the traders is the root from which the whole tragic sequence springs, for had not the priests, who remain to promise compensation and remonstrance, found in the traders a body whose livelihood was threatened by these proceedings, they would not have possessed a current of opposition with which eventually to turn the tide of His popularity. By this act, as Mr. Louis Wilkinson has rightly insisted, our Lord arrayed the monied interests and the business community against Him. Yet, as he adds, few plays show to us this encounter between a man's conscience and his work, or make *money* the decisive factor that it often is upon the struggle. Dathan, the chief of the traders, is the most eager for revenge, and the promise of

Nathaniel (a priest) to lay their complaint before the Sanhedrin, which closes the first act, prepares us for all that is to follow.

It seems to me essential to describe at least the opening scene in some detail, if only to show how vividly the contemporary atmosphere is recovered, and the skill with which the hints contained in the Gospel narrative, the more pregnant from their very brevity, are developed. I have also hoped by this means to let the reader understand how richly the text will reward his study.

But we must hurry on. The Sanhedrin natur- ally welcomes the one popular element that is still loyal, and, having decided that the innovator must be imprisoned, embraces Dathan's proposal to offer a large reward to one of the disciples for information concerning how He may be arrested secretly. The leave-taking at Bethany, which troubles all, is made especially to trouble Judas, who asks : " But, Master, what will become of us if Thou givest up Thy life ? "   His fears for him- self, and the welfare of the little band, of which he is the treasurer, are much increased by the " waste " of the precious ointment. You feel not only his fears for himself, should he be left leader- less, but that his worldly-wise sense of responsi- bility has been outraged. Who will take thought for us if I do not ? he says in self-defence. He had grown subdued to what he worked in, money and accounts, and these, from prudential motives, he has already occasionally manipulated to his own

advantage. These " savings," he tells us in
soliloquy, seem now to him his only security, and
he falls an easy prey to the suggestion of Dathan
that, since the Master has Himself foretold disaster, his future can be secured by earning the reward
now offered by the Sanhedrin. You hear this
money paid to him, for each coin is counted upon
a marble table, on which it rings. The bargain
is concluded, despite the protest of Nicodemus,
who, with St. Joseph of Arimathea, leaves the
Sanhedrin in indignation when the death of the
Betrayed is decided on. This want of unanimity
gives a convincing touch to the voting in the
council chamber.

The scene of the Last Supper is a living replica
of Leonardo da Vinci's picture. The washing of
the feet is performed for all. The first Mass is
said, and the Bread and Wine are presented to
each disciple, who severally receive, save that they
are seated, as communicants do to this day.
Nothing, except description, could destroy the
impressiveness of this scene.

But what may be described is the whisper in
which Judas, too, asks : " Lord, is it I ? " In the
agitation of the disciples who have cried aloud
these words, the subsequent whisper of Judas is
lost. You then notice that, had he also not asked
their question, he would have avowed himself.
His agitation, so different from their own, his
guilty whisper, so unlike their horrified appeal, is a
moment to be remembered.

Dathan and the traders accompany the Temple
guard, sent by the Sanhedrin at the request of
Judas, to the Garden.   Money, once aroused,
dogs the heels of Jesus to the end.   (It is suggestive, though it was, of course, because they were
receiving foreign pay, that the friendship of our
Lord for the publicans was made by the Jews a
charge against Him.)   The appearance of an
angel to lighten His solitude in the garden, for the
disciples slept at the moment when He was most
alone, lends that ray of light to the darkest hour,
the little good in the midst of great ill, which,
according to Aristotle, is the meaning of pathos.
After the tension of this scene, the arrest, with
which it ends, is almost a relief.   At this point our
four hours watch is over, and the first division ends.

The eighth act begins with the anxiety of the
High Priests, and especially of Annas, lest the
disturber of the peace should somehow have
escaped them.   The characters of Annas and
Caiaphas are well contrasted.   Caiaphas is a
vigorous personality, an ecclesiastical politician,
eager, active and determined.   Annas, now in old
age, has survived this stage of development to
become a frantic conservator of tradition.   The
preservation of the Law has become an obsession
with him.   He cannot die in peace so long as an
iota is imperilled.   The personal activity, no
longer his to exercise, oppresses him, and he can
trust no one, not even Caiaphas, to do all that he
himself would do, had he the power.   When Judas

brings the news of the arrest, Annas immediately
is consumed with desire to see the next step taken,
and his words, " Even before the Feast the
Galilean must die," are the first that reveal to
Judas how his treachery is to be made use of.   To
his passionate protest the priests coolly reply,
" Thou hast delivered Him over : the rest is our
business " ; and we see how Judas is already in
the toils.   We see next the scene before the fire
when Peter denies any knowledge of the prisoner,
and are wounded by the silent glance which Jesus
casts upon him as His arrival diverts the soldiers'
attention to Himself.   It is at such silent moments
that Anton Lang (the Christ of 1900, 1910 and
1922) is at his best.   We miss the note of triumph
in his entry to Jerusalem, but the notes of pity and
of suffering are his own.   The succeeding
tableau, representing the despair of Cain, pre-
figures the despair of Judas, whose part, played by
Guido Mayr, could not be better conceived.   The
very photograph of him is a revelation.   Nor can
the audience miss the poignant moment when, in
his last soliloquy before " the blasted tree," Judas
realizes that he has been called a traitor, not by
those that he betrayed, but by the paymasters to
whom he has betrayed them.   Paymasters and
politicians are all alike.

The scenes before Pilate were to me among the
great scenes in the play.   Hans Mayr, who played
the Procurator, looked the Roman, and made it
impossible not to realize what exceptional strength

would have been necessary to withstand the clamour to which at length he yielded, in spite of himself. Three times the Procurator evaded his pursuers, three times they doubled upon his tracks. The effect of the crowd supporting the priests is so tremendous that the courage Pilate did display is as striking as his final failure. Till the last moment, you cannot but believe that his Roman self-possession, respect for order, and contempt for lynch law, will baffle the fanatics who rage below his balcony like an infernal sea. His rebukes of their ferocity set Roman reason and Palestinian frenzy in fine contrast. We feel that his contempt for this unruly people was deserved. When they ask him not " to trouble himself " with a second investigation, but to confirm the death-sentence that they have already passed, he replies : " Do you dare to suggest to me, Cæsar's representative, that I should be a blind instrument for the execution of your orders ? I must know what law he has broken, and in what way." Dismayed by this rebuff, they repeat the charges of blasphemy, and refer to the entry into Jerusalem. To each the Procurator has a crushing answer, and when they mention Cæsar's name, he compliments them ironically upon their suddenly awakened zeal.

The private hearing is then ordered, because Pilate suggests to his attendants that when He is no longer confused by the fury of the crowd and His accusers, He will perhaps speak. The soldiers clear the court, and Jesus is led up the

steps to where Pilate has been standing. Pilate
then seats himself before the Prisoner, a little act
that is one of the fine moments of this scene.   In
the brief interview that follows, Pilate's historic
" Am I a Jew ? " shows all the Roman contempt
for the natives of his province, and his second
question, *Was ist Wahreit ?* which, perhaps, refers
only to our Lord's previous words, is neither con-
temptuous nor lightly spoken. The Roman believes that there is no absolute criterion ; consideration, rather than dogmatic scepticism,
prompts the words.   Telling his wife that he will
do all he can to save Him, Pilate again summons
the Jews :   " He has done nothing worthy of
death.   Punish Him according to your law, if He
has offended it."   When the priests say : " He
proclaims Himself a King," Pilate answers : " It
is openly taught among the Romans that every
wise man is a King."   Learning that He is a
Galilean, Pilate seeks a way of escape by sending
Him to Herod, because Galilee is in Herod's
jurisdiction.

The vulgar curiosity of the Tetrarch, who desires to be gratified by the sight of a miracle, is in
admirable contrast with the dignity of this preceding trial.   The Asiatic tyrant and the Roman
Procurator are a contrasting complement to each
other.   But Herod, too, sees in His simplicity a
nature incapable of crime.

Matters are now proving so unexpectedly difficult for the Jews that, on returning to Pilate, they

resolve to stake all upon an appeal to Cæsar, should he still refuse to give way.   Pilate next orders the scourging in an attempt to satisfy their rage, and then, accusing them of personal envy, appeals, over their heads, to the people who had acclaimed Jesus but five days before.   " The result of this," said Caiaphas with a smile, " will show, O Governor, that thou thinkest evil of us unjustly."   But Pilate cannot believe that the popular choice between Jesus and Barabbas is doubtful.   When Barabbas is chosen, his indignation knows no bounds ; for he is ignorant how the traders have been used by the priests to poison the crowd, and that it is not a mob but a carefully organized regiment.   Its turbulence is so great that Pilate's guard leaves his house suspecting an insurrection. The vast stage becomes a tossing sea.   And the cry, " His blood be upon us and upon our children," is as horrible as a fearful dream.

The realism, which grows ever more poignant, has now begun to dominate the scene ; and the crown of thorns is pressed downward by four soldiers with two crossed staves, as it may sometimes be seen in old pictures.   The staves bend like bows, and the silence can be felt.   The reading of the formal words, in which the official sentence is at last pronounced by Pilate's officer, is accompanied by the breaking of Pilate's staff which he then throws in horror among the multitude ; and the hideous exultation of Caiaphas makes him, and not Pilate, the evil genius of the scene.

The Way to Golgotha makes use of the peculiar structure of the stage, for, as the tumultuous procession crowds before us on the right, Mary and St. John appear upon the left.   Thus the inner stage prevents the pair from knowing the sight that awaits them.   Their terrible moment of suspense communicates itself to the audience, because the inner stage hides the two approaching parties from each other.   On no other stage could the moment of this meeting convey itself.   It is the inner stage that makes it possible, just as the want of it makes the meeting of the Montagus and Capulets unconvincing in a modern theatre.

The crucifixion at Ober-Ammergau must be seen to be believed.   Actors and audience are spared nothing, and the realism is made the more acute from the beauty in which it is set.   The colour and the grouping here, as throughout, are lovely, but, as in real life, those upon the stage are too busy to be aware of the parts they play, or the picture they make to the sun above them.   The scene takes us into the very arcanum of suffering, and the words " I thirst " and " Sabachthani " are as the voice of those silent sorrows that is heard only of God.   Then comes the order to break the bones of the crucified.   The soldier places his ladder against the cross to which each thief is tied, and, running lightly up it, with a heavy club strikes the two thigh bones and the shoulders of each, so that their bodies are twisted out of shape.   Then he takes a lance, and with the thrust blood and water spurt upon the ground. The surviving remnant of the Procurator's courage is seen in the inscription that he refuses to withdraw, and in his order that the Body shall be delivered to St. Joseph of Arimathea " As a gift from Pilate." Thus, at the eleventh hour, the priests feel foiled, and already taste the savour of the cup that the first Easter morning shall present to them.

The Resurrection and the Ascension are brief, calm scenes, the last of which has the fitting repose of a simple, motionless, tableau.

The introduction of Veronica on the way to Golgotha is the only notable departure from the written record, for though the dialogue has been expanded at a hundred points, and whole scenes written from perhaps half a verse, the play never seems to trespass beyond the limits of the Gospels. Looking backward upon it, at once a tragedy and a spectacle, as we see life itself in our crowded streets, we understand the artistic possibilities of a play described as a " history," and what may be gained by the sacrifice of the first two dramatic unities to concentrate all upon the third, which, if the chronicle-form be justified, embraces them.

Of the actors there is no need to speak in detail. At no moment is the representation forced, or insincere. The oldest actor began as a child in the crowd or in one of the tableaux. The tradition is in the blood of each. Anton Lang's *Christ* is the Christ (may we say ?) of pious devotion. He is best in his silence and endurance, but he lacks (who would not lack ?) the commanding quality that gave more than dignity, more than impressiveness, to His words. If it may be honestly said that there were no faults in the representation, save (one agrees) that the crowd too often speaks in unison, the virtues are intertissued with the words ; and that is why, in the attempt to make the reader aware of them, I have made a long draught upon his patience, hoping to take him with me through these eight hours, because no summary or conspectus is sufficient to convey the cumulative effect of the whole. After all is over, we have, as it were like St. Thomas, put our finger into each print of the nails, and become the contemporaries of the action, which remains in the memory as a piece of living history seen by one who was present all the time. That memory is the play's achievement, and till it shall have been communicated, remarks upon the significance or devotional uses of the drama seem to me idle and unreal. It is for the reader, as for the spectator, to draw them. Can the reader be enabled to do so ? I have attempted no more.

1922.

Note

The Passion Play at Ober-Ammergau, 1910. Full text, in German and English, copiously illustrated. Stead's Publishing House, Kingsway, London, 4*s*.

E

JOHN GAY

IT is much to be hoped that the revival of *The Beggar's Opera* has done neglected justice to the dramatic gifts of John Gay, and that the patrons of the Lyric Theatre, Hammersmith, will have studied the dialogue of the opera. The songs and the dialogue are excellent testimony to his gifts as a lyrist and a wit, and invite the discriminating reader to make closer acquaintance with his essays on " Dress " and " Reproof and Flattery " (which appeared in *The Guardian*, Nos. 11 and 149, 1712–13),[1] and with his ballads and verse in other pieces beside the popular *Fables*. It is odd that, though Gay has found friendly critics and devoted editors in John Underhill and Austin Dobson, neither of them speaks of his reputation without apology nor gives any convincing reasons for the original success of *The Beggar's Opera*. For example, John Underhill attributes the success of the

---

[1] The prose is accessible in *An English Garner* compiled anew by J. Churton Collins, where Gay's " The Present State of Wit " is reprinted, while the two pieces from *The Guardian* can be found in Volume III of John Bell's edition of Gay's *Works*, published in 1773.

opera to "two causes : the opera was the first
specimen of a new species of composition, and it
was well stored with satire. The satire, moreover, was not merely general : it was personal and
particular. No one could fail to see that Robin
of Bagshot—*alias* Whiff Bob, *alias* Carbuncle,
alias Bob Booty—was designed to represent Sir
Robert Walpole's unrefined manners, convivial
habits, and alleged robbery of the public. Macheath was provided in the play with both a wife
and mistress, to indicate to the public that Lady
Walpole had a rival in Miss Skerrett." The
simple and sufficient objection to the adequacy of
these two explanations is that the opera has drawn
multitudes to-day when neither any longer exists.
Nor was Austin Dobson much happier when,
after admitting that Gay " as a song writer is very
successful, his faculty in this way being greatly
aided by his knowledge of music," qualifies this
and his further acknowledgment of the additions
made by Gay to " well-known quotations," with
the remark that " those who read his *life* will
probably wonder at his poetical reputation even in
his own time." It seems clear, then, that, between extreme popularity and contemnation,
criticism has not told us what Gay's literary gifts
really were.

The explanation, perhaps, is that Gay's desire
of patronage and relative indolence have much
occupied his editors, who spend unnecessary time
in apologies for these traits in his character. But

his character is only one of the data ; it is not a
matter for eulogy or sermonizing.   Had it been
different, his work would have been different.   It
interests us now only because it helps to throw
some light upon his work.   His dramatic sense is
indicated by his promptitude to seize the occasion.
The Fan was written to celebrate a new fashion ;
The Mohocks to make dramatic use of a temporary
scare ; and the same desire to keep pace with the
moods of the moment involved Gay in the loss of
his fortune through the collapse of the South Sea
Bubble.   This editorial desire to apologize for
Gay (the excuse for which is to show that Gay
was not so badly treated as he and his friends
imagined) has set the critics on the wrong track.
It was surely a curious suggestion of Mr. Dobson
to refer readers to Gay's " life," instead of to his
works, for the source of his poetical reputation.
I propose here the simpler task of letting his works
justify themselves.

For this it really suffices to turn to the text of
The Beggar's Opera, since the recent revival will,
I think finally, have set that work above the
Fables, the continued popularity of which, at
the present day, is perhaps open to doubt.
Though the songs in *The Beggar's Opera* are the
most exquisite parts of that work, the dialogue
also is excellent, witty prose which, like the songs,
delights as much for its dramatic appropriateness
as for the deft touch and ready wit which distinguish it.   Let us be grateful to Austin Dobson

for drawing attention to Gay's accomplishment as a musician, since, though we can adduce no evidence but Warton [1] for this accomplishment, it is obvious from the songs themselves. They really sing, and that the singing quality in them is the proof of a rare technician becomes apparent when we remember that familiar tunes were chosen for their setting, which they were devised to fit. That is their first virtue, a learned grace. The second is the dramatic appropriateness of their matter. Every song has something to say, expressive of the character which sings it ; and this something is expressed so cleanly that there are no loose ends. The matter of the songs continually assists the progress of the action. In the third place, the art of the songs is varied. They are not only charming patterns of sound, deftly woven to suit the music, but so varied in design that they can start a rollicking chorus, touch the listener with pathetic words, or, again, merely delight us with witty and graceful cadences. Those who have witnessed the opera remember the tunes from the words, and there can be no finer tribute to a librettist. Thus, the rollicking music of the chorus :

[1] Warton (*Pope*, Vol. I, p. 149, 1797) wrote : " Pope, being insensible to the effects of music, inquired of Dr. Arbuthnot whether Handel really deserved the applause he met with. The Duchess of Queensberry told me that Gay could play on the flute, and that this enabled him to adapt so happily some airs in *The Beggar's Opera*."

> Let us take the road.
> Hark ! I hear the sound of coaches !
> The hour of attack approaches,
> To your arms, brave boys, and load !

rings anew in the ears with the printed words before us. Again, the charming song of pleading,
wherein Polly explains to her parents how she
came to give her hand to the highwayman, evokes
its delightful tune in the refrain :

> But he so teased me,
> And he so pleased me,
> What *I* did you must have done.

The accentuation of the words in these songs is
faultless. It falls always idiomatically as in lively
speech, so that in such a song as

> How happy could *I* be with either,
> Were t'other dear charmer away !

in the first line the emphasis falls beautifully upon
the personal pronoun, and there is no bungling of
the triple measure throughout. As actors say,
the words " carry over the footlights," and as such
are true dramatic speech. The songs also have a
pictorial quality. They bring the scenes before
us because the writer has seen these himself in the
clearest outline. What could better evoke the
scene of a farmyard than the song which accompanied the delicious ballet at the end of the second
act :

Before the barn-door crowing,
The cocks by hens attended,
His eyes around him throwing,
Stands for a while suspended.

Then one he singles from the crew,
And cheers the happy hen ;
With how d'you do, and how d'you do,
And how d'you do again.

An instance of a more complicated melody is seen in the following :

If the heart of a man is depressed with cares,
The mist is dispelled when a woman appears ;
Like the notes of a fiddle, she sweetly, sweetly,
Raises the spirits, and charms our ears.

Is not that third line enchanting with its repetition of the last word ? Does it not carry its own music in its lilt ? Now, hand on your heart, reader, have you ever read better songs in a musical comedy than those of which the above are a few samples ? Are they not as good on the boards as in the study, and do they not compare favourably with Gilbert's (being far richer in humanity than his) in the sense that they are equally light, while, unlike many of his, they do not depend for our applause upon the literary triviality of humour ? From Gay and Pepusch to Gilbert and Sullivan the artistic cycle of English light opera is complete.

Gay marries in these songs the several gifts of

the graceful lyrist and the dramatic directness of a
good playwright ; his lyrics are enriched by the
limits which the drama imposed on them.   As a
librettist of light opera he need fear no compari-
sons that we can make.   For the matter in the
songs, if not profound, is full of authentic good
sense, and of the rare wisdom which can take
itself lightly.   Let me quote but two examples :

> Youth's the season made for joys,
>   Love is then our duty ;
> She alone who that employs
>   Well deserves her beauty.
>   Let's be gay
>   While we may,
> Beauty's a flower despised in decay.

and this :

> 'Tis most certain,
>   By their flirting,
> Women oft have envy shown ;
>   Pleased to ruin
>   Others' wooing,
> Never happy in their own.

People must be very blind indeed if they fail to see
the excellent good sense that forms the substance
of this verse.   Indeed, when Macheath declares
that " nothing unbends the mind " so much as
women, we fancy that he must be quoting from
Coventry Patmore.   The wisdom and the wit are
the same, for wisdom is justified of *all* her children.
   The prose dialogue there is no space to praise,

though it fully justifies us to seek the few essays
and letters which Gay wrote.   His prose in these
and in *The Beggar's Opera* is written in witty and
idiomatic English, and we share John Underhill's
lament that Gay did not produce more prose.
For lack of it we must rest Gay's reputation as a
man of letters mainly upon *The Beggar's Opera*.
The *Fables*, I think, are losing, or will eventually
lose, their hold upon us, because the delight of the
fable is not one which permanently endears the
form to us.   No one seems to have noticed that the
germ of the *Fables* is the tale of the crow and the
lark which concludes the Epistolary Verses to
Methuen of 1720.   The *Fables* were not published till 1727.   There are moods when the
fable is delightful, but they are transient.   Even
Æsop and La Fontaine sometimes fail to move us,
for the fable, which is the proverb writ large, like
the proverb, hardly survives our first appreciation
of its point.   We may quote it for its aptness, like
a proverb, but we forget the author, since in fable
and proverb his personality seems to wither in the
narrow compass of his work.   We had rather
have the fable in the form of an essay, because in
the essay, side by side with the moral, the writer's
personality has room to breathe.   Gay's *Fables*,
then, enforce our appreciation of his quality as a
prose writer, and afford another reason for our
regret that so little prose came from his pen.
Apart from the songs of *The Beggar's Opera*, some
in *Polly* and in *Achilles*, beside *Black-eyed Susan*, not

much of his poetry need detain us.   In *The Fan*,
which Mr. Austin Dobson declared to be " un-
readable," the curious reader will note a resemblance to the famous rhapsody on clothes in *The
Angel in the House*.   The passages in *The Fan* are
the concluding lines of Book I, and lines 69–86 of
Book II.   Whether Patmore was indebted to
Gay is indeterminable, and of course Pope's *Rape
of the Lock* must not be forgotten.   The toilette
was the Muse's altar then.   Much of Gay's verse
has the fatal defect of being neither positively bad
nor really excellent, though even in *Rural Sports*
or *Trivia*,—for instance, the humorous couplet :

> Ask the grave tradesman to direct thee right,
> He ne'er deceives but when he profits by't—

but not in *Wine*, I could put my finger on lines
that remind us of what Gay could write at his best.
The real lessons to be learned from the revival of
his opera were that in Gay we have a delightful
lyrist whose matter and whose manner were perfectly married to the dramatic end which he had
in view, and, secondly, that a reprint of the few
examples of his admirable prose would be both
timely and deserved.

In justice to Gay we must remember that he
added the following famous quotations to our
speech :

> Over the hills and far away,

an improved variant on an earlier phrase of

D'Urfey, an author to whom Gay refers in the
" Wednesday " and " Friday " sections of *The
Shepherd's Week* :

> Brother, brother, we are both in the wrong.

> How happy could I be with either,
> Were t'other dear charmer away !

> In every age and clime we see
> Two of a trade can never agree,

to say nothing of his own famous epitaph :

> Life is a jest, and all things show it;
> I thought so once, but now I know it.

In sum, if Gay's reputation must rest upon but a
small part of his complete works, the part which
survives is as good as anything of its kind, and as a
writer of idiomatic dialogue and of songs for
actors in a play he is unrivalled. The difficulty
and rareness of this feat blind most people to its
quality, for an audience or a reader will listen to,
or read, a song merely for the song's sake, and
without appreciation of the place which it should
also occupy in the action. A song which satisfies
the actor as well as the audience is a song indeed,
and neither English verse nor the English stage is
rich in such pieces. It is tempting to add a word
on the charm of the opera itself which, for all the
artificiality of its construction, consists in an
escape from the conventions, and in the praise of
life as average human beings desire it. There is

genuine humanity in the characters, genuine desire in their desires, and such spontaneity in their naughtiness that the Pharisee in all of us is rebuked by their vitality.

If an anthology were compiled of Strict Prose, in the interest of that neglected art, Gay would have an important place in it. He would have to be set beside Swift and Congreve. A comparison of his dialogue with that of Congreve would reveal the fineness of Gay's ear. No one's dialogue is more idiomatic or more beautiful, and in modern drama this art is sadly neglected.

For example, it is safe to affirm that the current success of *The Man with a Load of Mischief* will not be repeated should the play be revived in future years, because, despite the merits of the idea, the charm of the period, the romance of the situation, the dialogue is so literary and stilted that it is all but impossible to speak. The cadence proper to be spoken and that proper to be read are as distinct as sound-rhymes and eye-rhymes in poetry. In acted drama dialogue must be tested by the ear, and the " literary play " is one which has been written unintentionally in a prose designed for reading. The two rhythms are distinct, and though conversational prose can be spoken or read with equal pleasure, the literary prose, conceived through the eye, is fatal eventually to acted drama. Since the primary appeal of the drama, however, is to the eye, from pantomime to the subtle shades of acting, the public, whose ears are gross, is easily misled, and often supposes itself to be enjoying poetry because the phrases to which it listens are awkward, stilted, and uncouth in sound. On this misconception the " literary play," with the help of costumes and a romantic setting, may momentarily thrive, while the true art of dialogue, of which Gay and Congreve were masters, endures because the appeal to the ear, in acted drama, is unfailing. A comparison, then, of the prose dialogue of *The Beggar's Opera* with the prose of *The Man with a Load of Mischief* enables the difference between cadence and prose, between the language of comedy and the literary play, to be recognized decisively. The acted play, like a jest, lives in the ear, for the ear is the final arbiter of idiom.

PEACOCK THE EPICUREAN

OF the lesser personalities which cannot be left out of the literary histories, Thomas Love Peacock will always be one. But, indeed, though this is true of his rank, it is less than true of his reputation. He remains free from the ups and downs of fashion, and in each generation he continues to live in the affections of a small but discriminating circle, which finds unusual refreshment in the vigour of his style and in the idiosyncrasy of his character. He preserves the crisp flavour of an English russet apple, whose rough rind conceals a sharp but sweet savour, as agreeable to the palate as it is to the teeth. As the friend and executor of Shelley, and the father-in-law of George Meredith, he is the subject of many passing references ; but as a man of letters he survives upon his merits as the inventor of the conversational novel. His father, Samuel Peacock, was a glass merchant of London, who died when Thomas was some three years old. His mother, Sarah, the daughter of Thomas Love, a naval captain, is chiefly known to us by one suggestive fact. Her son was so much devoted to her, that her death in 1833 is said to have discouraged him from further writing. He showed to her all he wrote and relied upon her sympathy and criticism. On the death of Peacock, senior, Mrs. Peacock and her son joined Captain Love at Chertsey ; and in the Abbey House, near by, Peacock, according to *Some Recollections of Early Childhood*, published in 1835, found the setting for the halls, castles, and abbeys of his later novels. He was sent to school at Englefield Green, where he acquired a love of learning so sincere that, though his schooldays were unusually brief, he made himself, in time, a sound classical scholar. In her biographical introduction to the three-volume edition of his works, which appeared in 1875, Peacock's granddaughter, Edith Nicholls, gives, in his own words, the following account of his education :

"I passed many of my best years with my mother, taking more pleasure in reading than in society. I was early impressed with the words of Harris : ' To be competently skilled in ancient learning is by no means a work of insuperable pains. . . . It is certainly as easy to be a scholar as a gamester or many other characters equally illiberal and low. The same application, the same quantity of habit, will fit us for one as completely as for the other.' Thus encouraged, I took to reading the best books, illustrated by the best critics ; and among the latter I felt specially indebted to Heyne and Hermann. Such was my education."

We next hear of him at the age of fourteen as a clerk in the firm of Ludlow, Fraser & Co., Throgmorton Street ; and while there he won an extra prize for an essay published in *The Monthly Preceptor*, a magazine for children which began in 1800. The subject of the essay was, " Is History or Biography the more improving Study ? " Leigh Hunt was a successful competitor ; but Peacock received an extra prize for the precocity of his performance, which, unfortunately, was written in verse. At no time is Peacock's life very rich in biographical matter, but the facts and the inferences to be drawn from them have been carefully collated by Mr. A. Martin Freeman, whose study of Peacock, published in 1911, is probably exhaustive in regard, at all events, to the originals for the characters of the novels.

After about two years in London, when he spent his spare time studying the classics in the British Museum, Peacock and his mother seem to have returned to Chertsey, where they lived upon her private means in studious leisure. Peacock divided his time between reading, the river, and a series of not very interesting attempts in verse. In 1804 he wrote *The Monks of St. Mark*, a boisterous ballad (a favourite form of poetry with him), in which his two typical motives of the bottle and the friar were characteristically combined. Two years later *Palmyra and Other Poems* appeared. The book is now remembered because Shelley, in one of his letters, gave it a word of superlative praise. But Mr. Freeman points out, in justice to both poets, that Shelley read the poem in the second edition of 1812, wherein the conclusion which had attracted his notice had been entirely changed. This edition, says the same authority, has never been reprinted. On these and the succeeding poems I do not propose to linger. The true Peacock is not to be found in them. By a happy chance the poems which show him at his best are to be found in the novels. Peacock made a false start. To pursue it in a short essay would be uncritical.

In the same year in which his volume of verse appeared Peacock made a walking tour in Scotland. He went alone, as was his habit ; and these solitary excursions, now in Scotland and later in Wales (he never travelled), stored his mind with those impressions which, as we shall shortly see, make his descriptions of scenery at once vivid and pleasing. Between 1806 and 1812 appeared *The Genius of the Thames*, a descriptive and reflective poem in the eighteenth-century manner, and three dramas which remained in manuscript till 1910, when they were printed with a preface by Dr. A. B. Young, in time for Mr. Martin Freeman to note them.

The year 1812 is more memorable for the

meeting with Shelley, to whom Peacock was
probably introduced by Edward Hookham, the
publisher, than for *The Philosophy of Melancholy*,
Peacock's next ambitious attempt in verse.   But
even the best of these attempts, *Rhododaphne*,
which appeared later, in 1818, has only the virtues
that remain when poetic inspiration is wanting :
fluidity of phrase, elegance, form—in short, the
qualities of a prose which has been made to
measure.   His experience for six months as
under-secretary to Sir Hope Popham, at Flushing,
during the winter of 1808–9, was a false start
in another direction.   The meeting with Shelley,
though it offers little material, was, however, the
turning-point in Peacock's literary life.   The
two men, scholarly in their tastes and affectionate
in their disposition, were mutually stimulating.
Peacock's wit, good-fellowship, and genial scepticism, were as attractive to Shelley as Shelley's
opinions and ideals were to him.   Each appealed
to the tolerance of the other through a scholarly
community of taste ; and in the Shelley circle
Peacock found a crowd of enthusiasts whose
" fervour " not only afforded him endless amuse-
ment, but gave him models for the opinionated
crew whose discussions were to be the staple
of his novels.   " Harriet Shelley was always
ready to laugh with me," Peacock recorded in his
subsequent recollections, " and we thereby lost
caste with some of the more hot-headed of the
party."   After his visit to Peacock in his old

age, Robert Buchanan records that Peacock
preferred Harriet to Mary Shelley, " if only on
the ground of her surpassing beauty." Is it
possible that Harriet had also the keener sense of
humour ?

It is with the publication of *Headlong Hall* in
1816 that Peacock made his first original contri-
bution to English letters. There had been
nothing like it before. There has been little
like it since, unless we care to mention Mallock's
New Republic. It is, perhaps, the most familiar
of the seven, of which Lord Houghton says that
they resemble more a French *conte* than anything
else.

To me they suggest a Platonic dialogue as
Aristophanes might have caricatured it, provided
that he had spared the cellar from his satire.
They are long short-stories, interspersed with
songs and lyrics, and, with two apparent excep-
tions, satires on contemporary opinion. With
little attempt at character or humanity, as a
rule not much plot, they interest us for the wit
of the dialogue which occupies the major part of
them and for their descriptions of scenery. The
scenery, indeed, is the only part of the structure
of the novels which is never reduced to absurdity.
To collect a gathering of persons with the latest
views upon contemporary subjects of discussion,
to set them in a country house with an ample
larder, and to dismiss them when they had
emptied on each other's heads their several vials

of opinion, was Peacock's usual proceeding.   We
have only to imagine a modern frequenter of,
say, the Fabian Summer School, recording the
discussions and arguments between Mr. Socialist,
Miss Artandcraft, Professor Psychoanalysis, and
Mr. Cubist, to see where and among whom, at
the present time, Peacock would have found a
setting for his satires.   In *Headlong Hall* a
bibulous Welsh squire entertains one Christmas
a party of philosophers, theorists, and critics,
each of whom is the walking embodiment of
one particular fad in diet or ideal.   Mr. Escot,
the deteriorationist ; Mr. Foster, the perfecti-
bilian ; Mr. Jenkinson, the statuquoite ; and
the Rev. Doctor Gaster, the gastrosoph, are the
chief.   It says much for the crispness of the
dialogue that we are interested in the speeches,
even though each speaker's name is a guide to
his ensuing words.   The following is an example
of their talk :
  " Mr. Escot : Clearly the correct interpreta-
tion of the fable of Prometheus is a symbolical
portraiture of that disastrous epoch when man
first applied fire to culinary purposes, and thereby
surrendered his liver to the vulture of disease.
From that period the stature of mankind has been
in a state of gradual diminution, and I have not
the least doubt that it will continue to grow small
by degrees and lamentably less, till the whole
race will vanish imperceptibly from the face of
the earth.

" Mr. FOSTER : I cannot agree in the consequences being so very disastrous.   I admit that
in some respects the use of animal food retards,
though it cannot materially inhibit the per-
fectibility of the species. . . ."

In the controversy concerning animal and
vegetable food, said Mr. Jenkinson, there is much
to be said on both sides ; and the question being
in equipoise, I content myself with a mixed
diet, and make a point of eating whatever is
placed before me, provided it be good of its
kind.

After further argument, Dr. Gaster declares
Mr. Jenkinson's conclusion to be orthodox.
Indeed, he adds, the *loaves and fishes* are typical
of a mixed diet.

Mr. Escot was in love with Miss Cranium
but had offended her father, the phrenologist,
whose complexion, at the sight of their mutual
blushes, " underwent several variations, from the
dark red of the peony to the deep blue of the
convolvulus."   During a walk Mr. Milestone,
the landscape gardener, and Mr. Gall, the critic,
discuss the nature of the picturesque :

" Mr. GALL : I distinguish the picturesque
and the beautiful, and I add to them, in the
laying out of grounds, a third and distinct
character, which I call unexpectedness.

" Mr. MILESTONE : Pray, sir, by what name
do you distinguish this character, when a person
walks round the grounds a second time ? "

There can hardly be a better instance of a good debating point, for the retort is, of course, a verbal victory only.   It should be added that in the later novels the dialogue is not so mechanical, and even one-idea enthusiasts are allowed to be sometimes illogical.   Were the matter not inter-esting, the stilted language would be fatal ; but the " Conversational Novel " has nothing in common either with conversation or with prose narrative.   It descends from the Socratic Dia-logue, wherein neither talk nor humanity (as the novelist knows them) professes to have part.

The year after the publication of *Headlong Hall*, Peacock's most original novel appeared under the title of *Melincourt*.   He had always been haunted by a picture of an orang-outang, which he had seen in his boyhood, and, as his custom was, he had read all that he could about its habits. The arguments of Lord Monboddo, an eighteenth-century evolutionist, who appears to have been somewhat overlooked, particularly impressed him. Peacock therefore decided to make this creature the hero of a novel, and to give chapter and verse for all his feats.   He set about his task in an exuberant and learned way.   The scholarly re-cluse, Mr. Sylvan Forester, the inhabitant of Redrose Abbey, explains to an old friend, who was paying him a visit, how the taciturn gentleman " with the ludicrous physiognomy ' set off ' by a pair of enormous whiskers," became a member of his household.   Mr. Oran, as he then was, had been purchased from a retired naval captain, who had bought him from a negro upon the coast of Angola, brought him home, taught him gardening, and to disport himself upon the flute and the French horn. Authorities for these and all his other accomplishments are quoted at length, and perhaps have won several readers for the ingenious and learned Lord Monboddo :

" ' With a view to ensuring him the respect of society which always attends rank and fortune,' Mr. Forester went on, ' I have purchased him a baronetcy, and made over to him an estate. I have also purchased from the Duke of Rotten-burgh one-half of the elective franchise vested in the body of Mr. Christopher Corporate, the free, fat, and independent burgess of the ancient and honourable borough of One-vote, who returns two members of Parliament, one of whom will shortly be Sir Oran Haut-ton.' Mr. Forester's friend whistled."

The difficulty of presenting such a character and of making him interesting is obvious enough, but Sir Oran was also dumb ! He had to convince by his actions and by his silence. This he does, and remains, on the fantastic plane, the most original conception in our fiction. In the recorded habits of his tribe, Peacock found sufficient for his purpose ; and Sir Oran rescues a lady, belabours a crowd, and carves a pheasant so convincingly that we never miss his want of speech.   Against the background of his silence all his actions become significant.   Our imagination waits upon him and is never disappointed. The story, from which, alas, he is inclined to disappear, is never more interesting than when he is present.

The heroine of *Melincourt* is one of Peacock's favourite women, with a mind of her own, a standard of her own, and the charm, at all events, of independence, generosity, and candour.   Even in her stilted style of speech, from which the " good women " of most of our novelists rarely escape, Anthelia Melincourt is curiously like Lydia in *Cashel Byron's Profession*.   She is supposed to have gained her freedom-loving soul from her upbringing in Westmorland, which is described as follows :

" The majestic forms and wild energies of nature that surrounded her from her infancy impressed their character on her mind communicating to it all their own wildness, and more than their own beauty.   Far removed from the pageantry of courts and cities, her infant attention was awakened to spectacles more interesting and more impressive : the misty mountain-top, the ash-fringed precipice, the gleaming cataract, the deep and shadowy glen, and the fantastic magnificence of the mountain clouds.   The murmur of the woods, the rush of the winds, and the tumultuous dashing of the torrents, were the first music of her childhood."

After this it is hardly surprising that her notion of a lover is extremely exacting. She sketches her requirements with the ardour and forensic eloquence of a practised public speaker. But, despite these artificial handicaps, she is attractive and sincere.

In the chapter called " The Torrent " is this description of a mountain storm :

" Suddenly the grey mist fled before the rising wind, and a deep black line of clouds appeared in the west, that, rising rapidly, volume on volume, obscured in a few minutes the whole face of the heavens. There was no interval of preparation, no notice for retreat. The rain burst down in a sheeted cataract, comparable only to the bursting of a waterspout. The sides of the mountains gleamed at once with a thousand torrents. Every little hollow and rain-worn channel, which but a few minutes before was dry, became instantaneously the bed of a foaming stream. Every half-visible rivulet swelled to a powerful and turbid river. . . . Anthelia looked back, and found herself on the solitary rock insulated on the swelling flood.

[A stranger suddenly appeared among the trees of the pine grove, and made gestures to show his willingness to help.]

" He paused a moment as if measuring with his eyes the breadth of the chasm, and then, returning to the grove, proceeded very deliberately to pull up a pine. Anthelia thought him mad ; but infinite was her astonishment to see the tree sway and bend beneath the efforts of his incredible strength, till at length he tore it from the soil, and bore it on his shoulders to the chasm."

Sir Oran had come upon the scene ; and his action is supported upon three footnotes from Rousseau, *Ancient Metaphysics*, and the *Letter of a Bristol Merchant ;* these declare, in effect, that he could pull up a whole forest if he chose, and we are perfectly ready to believe them.

But as the novel proceeds it becomes increasingly discursive and argumentative, though it is relieved by the stirring episode of the election, and the lively description of the chairing of the new M.P.s, unfortunately too long to quote. Peacock's intolerance of mysticism and his chaff of Mr. Mystic remind me of a modern Hellenist who confessed that Coleridge's *Aids to Reflection* had been a severe hindrance to himself. Such another Hellenist was Peacock, Peacock the Epicurean ! Were common sense, as the term is ordinarily used, based upon sufficient reflection and knowledge, it would be no bad equivalent for the wisdom of the ancients. They accepted life as they found it, and, while distinguishing between common sense and vulgar prejudice, used reflection to make the most of life on a foundation of possible virtue and reasoned morals. Peacock is best described as a Tory, with a Tory's characteristic independence and hatred of shams

and abuses, wherever found. His apparently
radical outbursts are nothing more than this Tory
independence.   His fund of common sense needs
no single spokesman, and, added to his quick
satirical intelligence, provides a pervasive influence throughout his novels ; it hovers here and
there among the characters, being more human
than any of them, and comes to us at last in the
flesh and blood of a set of prejudices, more human
and more convincing than anything colder than
themselves.

There is more plot in Peacock's third novel,
Nightmare Abbey, which appeared in 1818.   It
has acquired some extrinsic popularity because
the melancholy Scythrop has been identified with
Shelley, though this adds little, I think, to our
enjoyment of the hero or his model.   It was the
" lightness, chastity, and strength " of the prose
in this novel which Shelley praised.   The melancholy Scythrop, with the *Sorrows of Werther* in his
hand, " built many castles in the air, and peopled
them with secret tribunals and bands of illu-
minati. . . . As he intended to institute a perfect
republic, he invested himself with absolute sover-
eignty over these mystical dispensers of liberty."
Mr. Flosky, the critic, wrapped in transcendental
gloom, anticipates the Erewhonian defence of
hypothetics by his belief in abstract reasoning and
his assault upon light, " the great enemy of
mystery."   He therefore christened his son
Emanuel Kant !   A humorous character is Mr.

Asterias, the ichthyologist, who has christened *his* son Aquarius.

Mr. Asterias believed in the existence of mermaids and tritons, whom he described as " the orang-outangs of the sea " a reminder of the motive which Peacock had put to original use in *Melincourt*. The belief of Mr. Asterias is supported by a learned argument, which reminds us that Peacock found most of his whimsies in scientific treatises and learned works. The knowledge thus gained made Peacock a master of the footnote, and he is one of the few writers, perhaps the only novelist, whose footnotes could not possibly be spared.

The plot provides this novel with a climax. It ends with the sound of unexpected and indeed arbitrary wedding bells. *Nightmare Abbey* also contains the capital drinking-song, wherein Mr. Hilary and the Rev. Mr. Larynx participated :

> Seamen three ! What men be ye ?
> Gotham's three wise men we be.
> Whither in your bowl so free ?
> To take the moon from out the sea.
> The bowl goes trim. The moon doth shine.
> And our ballast is old wine.
> And your ballast is old wine.

Peacock's humour, which had its root in reverence, approves Dr. Johnson's dictum that he who does not mind his belly will hardly mind anything else. Except for Meredith and, I am told,

Mr. John Galsworthy, this epicure's delight in
good cheer, the sacrament of hospitality, has van-
ished from our novels.   Cellars have passed
either into the female line, with the usual disastrous consequences, or shrunk to the dimensions
of a small cupboard.   It is remarkable that diet-
etics, about which we know so little, have usurped
the " Physiologie du Goût " about which we have
inherited so much.   Yet I must feelingly record
that the only occasion when I have been offered
Steinberg Cabinet was at the table of a notorious
teetotaller.

Peacock had now reached the age of thirty-
three.   With several volumes of verse, of which
he must have begun to feel the limitations, and
three respectfully received but not very successful
novels, he had reached a time when it became
necessary to ask himself if he had really found his
feet either in life or in letters.   It must have been
difficult not to reply in the negative.   So he
began to reconsider his position.   A former
schoolfellow of his, Peter Auber, happened to be
secretary to the East India Company, and apparently procured Peacock a nomination.   The
company is credited with keeping an open-eye
for young men of ability, which it was prepared
to test by examination.   After a few months'
study Peacock appeared before the examiners,
who marked his papers " Nothing superfluous
and nothing wanting," and was appointed an
assistant examiner, under James Mill, whom he

succeeded eighteen years later.　He promptly married Jane Gryffiths, a Welsh girl whom he had met eight years before.　In his administrative work Peacock showed great ability.　He was an early believer in the iron steamboat, a redoubtable witness before Parliamentary Committees, and received the praise of General F. R. Chesney for the model instructions which he drafted for the Euphrates Expedition of 1835. In 1836 he became chief examiner, and twenty years later retired upon a pension.

In the office of the East India Company he found scope for all his gifts ; so robust a personality could hardly fail to be a capable administrator ; and we cannot doubt that his literary gifts made his official reports admirable and tonic reading.　Such people, and we may include Florence Nightingale among the number, are born writers of text-books, being no less admirable presenters of facts than they are critics of theory.

But he did not at once abandon the habit of writing novels.　His next two, *Maid Marian* (1822) and *The Misfortunes of Elphin* (1829), can be conveniently taken together, for they were his sole excursions into the land of romance.　We do not think of Peacock rejoicing in Sherwood Forest or at home in prehistoric Wales ; but these two novels, especially *Maid Marian*, are, I think, better reading than their predecessors, perhaps because his characters, being semi-historical, could not be so opinionated as their modern counterparts. Robin Hood is the hero of *Maid Marian* ; and the charm of the book is well described by Lord Houghton in the excellent criticism which he contributed to the three-volume edition mentioned above. Its atmosphere, he says, is " a kind of compromise between the old Greek freedom and the Christianity of the Middle Ages." Its scene is so vivid, and the story moves with so little disturbance, that it was made into an opera by Planché, and " produced with great success at Covent Garden." Bishop, Peacock's grand-daughter records, composed the music, and " Charles Kemble made a great hit with one song, the only one in his career that he ever learnt to sing." The hearty friars of Rubygill Abbey are drawn with appropriate rosiness, much perhaps as they were regarded by the less censorious in the days when the religious orders had become a profession more of profit than of faith. They discuss dinner, in both senses, very well :

" The good qualities of a trout, said the little friar, are firmness and redness : the redness, indeed, being the sign of all the other virtues.

" Whence, said Brother Michael, we choose our abbot by his nose."

Among the songs are :

It was a friar of orders free,
A friar of Rubygill.

And the even better :

> Though I be now a grey, grey friar,
>   Yet I was once a hale young knight:
> The cry of my dogs was the only choir
>   In which my spirit did take delight.
>
> Little I recked of matin bell,
>   But drowned its toll with my clanging horn:
> And the only beads I loved to tell
>   Were the beads of dew on the spangled thorn.

The story is spiced rather than interrupted by its satire, which is insinuated by the way. Thus :
" So Robin and Marian dwelt and reigned in the forest, ranging the glades and the green woods from the matins of the lark to the vespers of the nightingale, and administering natural justice according to Robin's ideas of rectifying the inequalities of human condition : raising the genial dews from the bags of the rich and idle, and returning them in fertilizing showers on the poor and industrious : an operation which more enlightened statesmen have happily reversed, to the unspeakable benefit of the community."

The novel ends with a charming scene in which Maid Marian fences with a strange knight, who proves to be King Richard, Cœur de Lion. Robin is restored to his Earldom of Huntingdon till the usurpation of King John sends him and Maid Marian back to Sherwood again. It would make a pretty stage tableau. But since it has already suggested an opera, composers in search

of a libretto might do worse than use the old
tale of *Daphnis and Chloe*, which Wilde was once
asked to dramatize for the music of the late Mr.
Dalhousie Young, or the *Romantic Adventures of a
Milkmaid*, by Thomas Hardy.   Best of all perhaps is the beautiful legend of *Caeneus and Caenis*
that Mr. E. P. Warren has re-created in his
volume of Greek stories published by Blackwell.

In *The Misfortunes of Elphin*, political criticism
is more intensive and culminates in the astonishing defence of the neglect of the great wall, set
against the sea, which the legendary Welsh custo-
dians justified on the ground that " the parts
that are rotten give elasticity to those which are
sound."   This was Canning's argument against
the reform of the British Constitution !   The
novel contains the best of all Peacock's songs, the
" War-song of Dinas Vawr," which " is put on
record as being the quintessence of all the war-
songs that were ever written, and the sum and
substance of all the appetencies, tendencies, and
consequences of military glory " :

> The mountain sheep are sweeter,
> But the valley sheep are fatter ;
> We therefore deemed it meeter
> To carry off the latter.
> We made an expedition ;
> We met a host and quelled it ;
> We forced a strong position,
> And killed the men who held it.

.   .   .   .   .   .

> We there, in strife bewild'ring,
> Spilt blood enough to swim in ;
> We orphaned many children,
> And widowed many women.
> The eagles and the ravens
> We glutted with our foemen ;
> The heroes and the cravens,
> The spearmen and the bowmen.

.   .   .   .   .   .

The inundation of Gwaelod when a terrific storm drives the sea through the wall, whose foundations have long crumbled through generations of neglect, is a piece of vivid narrative and true comic description. Seithenyn ap Seithyn was carousing with his companions, and at the crashing of the walls and the invasion of the waters, cried : " Show me the enemy " in the perfection of drunken ineptitude.

All these novels, except perhaps *Melincourt*, which is also the longest, have the quality of asides, or recreations, or experiments. We cannot imagine the writer devoting his life to them, and no doubt he felt freer to indulge his pen when he was once happily established in the India Company's office.

In 1831 Peacock published *Crotchet Castle*, the last of the early novels, and then ceased for twenty-nine years. While it differs neither in title, scheme, nor manner from its predecessors, *Crotchet Castle* possesses a peculiar character of its own. The Welsh scenery and the love-story

unfolded there seem to reflect more directly
than the other novels Peacock's own life.   Jane
Gryffiths, his future wife, was first met in his solitary
rambles there, and the portrait of the heroine of
this story has a personal touch which distinguishes
her among his heroines.   Here also we meet the
Rev. Dr. Folliott, an epicure of such taste that he
can lay down the law even about breakfast, a meal
to which most aristologists devote very little
attention, perhaps because it is the only one that
even sociable souls can enjoy alone without re-
proach.   But to my mind the real distinction of
Crotchet Castle is that it contains Peacock's one
true poem : " In the Days of Old " :

> In the days of old,
> Lovers felt true passion,
> Deeming years of sorrow
> By a smile repaid.
> Now the charms of gold,
> Spells of pride and fashion,
> Bid them say good-morrow
> To the best-loved maid.
>
> Through the forests wild,
> O'er the mountains lonely,
> They were never weary
> Honour to pursue :
> If the damsel smiled
> Once in seven years only,
> All their wanderings dreary
> Ample guerdon knew.

Now one day's caprice
Weighs down years of smiling,
Youthful hearts are rovers,
Love is bought and sold :
Fortune's gifts may cease,
Love is less beguiling ;
Wiser were the lovers
In the days of old.

The beautiful old metre exactly suits the sentiment ; and if we compare this poem with the
better-known " Love and Age " (the sentiment is
not dissimilar), I think we shall agree that, except
in his drinking songs, Peacock was not safe with
the long line, if his rill was not to run into the
sands. " Love and Age," human as it is, rum-
bles on with the movement of an omnibus. The
heart of the matter is there, the movement and
the music are not.

The long silence which followed the publication of *Crotchet Castle* was filled with Peacock's
administrative work for the India Office, though
he occasionally took up his pen, for instance, to
write musical articles for the *Globe* and the
Examiner, to review very slashingly Moore's
novel *The Epicurean*, and to publish recollections
of Shelley.

In his final novel, *Gryll Grange*, Peacock expressed his musical opinions, his dislike of com-
petitive examinations, his scepticism of flint
instruments, his admiration of Greek music and
painting, through the mouth of the Rev. Dr.

Opimian, the most genial of all his clerics, and
the obvious precursor of Meredith's Dr. Middle-
ton. The character and household of Mr.
Falconer, who lives a studious life in an old tower
waited on by seven vestals, are a genuine creation.
So is the amiable Lord Curryfin, the one amusing
oddity in the novels who never forfeits Peacock's
affection or our own. Miss Gryll and the statu-
esque Miss Niphet are also human beings, who
make excellent foils to one another. *Gryll Grange*
and *Melincourt* have more individual character
than the other novels, which, in memory, it is
difficult to distinguish from one another.

Casting back over the whole series, we do not
trace much development, and are forced to regard
the Peacock novel as the occasional literary relax-
ation of a man of scholarly tastes who was also a
man of action. So far as I am aware, Lord
Houghton remains the best critic of Peacock, and
I cannot do better than conclude with a quotation
from his Preface to the edition of 1875. Since
it is Peacock's clergy who linger chiefly in our
memories, we may take Lord Houghton's judgment on them as a just and convenient farewell.
After noting the " total absence of theology " in
the conversation of these clergy, their sound
scholarship, their Tory tastes, their humour and
love of good cheer, Lord Houghton defines their
relation to the other clergy in English fiction.
Peacock's, he says, " is, in fact, the transition view
of the position of the sacerdotal class in this coun-

try that lay between the caricatures or pastorals
of apostolic simplicity in Parson Adams and the
Vicar of Wakefield and the very different notions
that have prevailed down to our own time . . .
all agreeing in isolating the clerical condition
from that of the rest of humanity "—he means in
expecting from them a sub-human manner of
life.   Since then the separation had grown so
wide that the clergy of fiction on or off the stage
became a wearisome absurdity.   Who is really
amused by Canon Chasuble, and who not grateful for the reaction which produced, for example,
the Rev. Mavor Morrell, Peter Keegan, and the
Bishop of Chelsea ?   Peacock's clergy show continuously less of caricature from Dr. Gaster to Dr.
Opimian.   To some extent this is true of all Peacock's characters.   Limited as his art was, we
cannot deny it some growth.

From first to last Peacock remained himself,
like a vintage wine, acquiring mellowness with
years : a link between the eighteenth and nineteenth centuries, greater than his books, but
difficult to conceive without them, in his old age a
fit object for such a literary pilgrimage as Robert
Buchanan has recorded in his *Poet's Sketch-Book.*
In Peacock the scholar, the man of action, and the
writer were very happily combined.   When we
think of him it seems a very English product ;
and, turning from his writings to the man himself, we meet a character that wins our affection
and admiration.   If salt is to be judged by its

sapidity, Peacock was one of the salt of the earth, whose Attic savour the world would be the poorer for losing. Happily, it still seasons our letters in the potency of Professor Saintsbury, and invigorates our taste through the sympathies of Edmund Gosse ; though, compared with such potent leaven as theirs, the Peacock sauce may seem—to our less catholic critics—a relish special to the few.

His fate was to be an intellectual foil to the contemporary Romantic school, and to remind men by his sound learning and keen humour that the sublime is rarely good sense, and that the best use of Romantic art is negative : to correct the formalism to which the classic tradition is periodically liable. Between the " intense inane " of Shelley's or Blake's philosophies of feeling and the barren materialism of Macaulay's actual world, Peacock the Epicurean stands like a pillar on behalf of the humanities at the place where sense and sensibility meet.

TWO FOOT-NOTES ON PATMORE

I. PATMORE AND DIVORCE

NOW that, thanks to Mr. Frederick Page's devoted researches, which are placing all future students of Coventry Patmore's early prose in his disciple's debt, the poet's unreprinted and often anonymous writings are being quietly identified, collected and published by the Oxford University Press, it is becoming possible to track the thought of the poet on a number of related questions, divagations of his central theme : to which last alone his principal writings were strictly dedicated.   We had, indeed, the gem : Mr. Page has now provided us with its radiations and their setting.

When we consider the Laureate of Wedded Love, as Edmund Gosse has called him, the most important of these questions seems to be undoubtedly that of divorce.   But until the first fruits of Mr. Page's investigations had been made available in *Courage in Politics*, the most authoritative pronouncement of Coventry Patmore upon divorce was, I think, an aphorism contained in *The Rod*,

The Root and The Flower : a piece of meditative
prose so exquisite in the quality of its thought
and in the sensitiveness of its diction that, naturally enough, it is read or even known by very few.
Among the Aurea Dicta that form the opening
section of this work, the CXXXVth declares a
little enigmatically :

" Love is a recent discovery, and requires a new
law. Easy divorce is the vulgar solution. The
true solution is some undiscovered security for
true marriage."

For the general reader this pronouncement requires the analysis of a modest word. Patmore
calls love a " recent discovery " because, as he
explains in one of the Preludes to *The Angel*, the
history of love is the history of man's fumbling
attempts at civilization ; and, since the days of
marriage by capture and the physical servitude of
the captured wife, love's recognition as the sub-
limation of desire is a relatively recent event in
human history.

The second sentence of the aphorism quoted
implies that the recognition of love to be apart
from desire is yet far from complete in the farmyard state of man's emotions, and, being thus
confused, love requires a solution of its present
awkward age of unsolved difficulties. For these
" easy divorce is the vulgar solution," because
the two words " popular " and " vulgar " are,
in etymology (as we all know), identical in
meaning.

Patmore, however, rejects easy divorce : to look
instead to " some undiscovered security for true
marriage." By this, as other references explain,
he means that human love, after the first movement
in which an instinctive election has been made, is
immediately beset with difficulties because each
lover is not the substance but the shadow of the
Reality whereof either makes the other aware.
(Love's " home is not here " ; Love is God ; and
of His love human love is the rehearsal and precursor only.) While this elementary distinction
is in process of being painfully apprehended by the
lovers, " the halo leaves the sacred head," and, in
the reaction of disappointment (a disappointment
divinely ordained in order to prove to humanity
that human love is *not*, and is not intended to be,
its " final good "), each lover is tempted to feel and
to declare human love to be an illusion, and
each lover, in his or her first bitterness, is tempted
further to disrupt the relation : in order, very
curiously, to invite a second disappointment elsewhere. It is curious that love should blind men
to the added complications that it brings to
human relations. Practically no people can live
permanently together without the friction caused
by constant nearness. If this be true of those
bound only by circumstances and uncomplicated
by emotional states of feeling, inference and
experience agree that love will prove an added
source of quarrels.

This is the root of the demand for divorce, a

demand that goes much deeper than the hard cases
employed to plead for it.   Patmore, in secular
terms, was not content with divorce because he
felt human love to be an initiation into a relation
larger than itself ; therefore he was also at an angle
to perceive, first, that the initiation could not win
its reward until it should have been persisted in
(since love is an adventure and, like all adventures
worthy of the name, love finds its quality only in
the heroic endurance of perils) ; and, second, that
just as the act of falling in love was an adventure of
faith, an arbitrary preference for one over numerous others that no ratiocination can justify or even
excuse, so also this adventure of faith reaps its
reward only by perseverance in the quest to which
the original flash of insight had beckoned it so
magically.

Thus illuminated by reference to his other writings, Patmore's aphorism from *The Rod, The Root
and The Flower* becomes intelligible, and explains
why he thought divorce to be a " vulgar," or inade-
quate solution of the need.   To this point his
collected works had carried the argument, but left
it there (apparently ignoring the difficulties and
hard cases) until Mr. Page's researches provided,
in a sense unexpectedly, the illustration previously
wanting :   the application of the argument on
the issue of an historical test case.

In *Courage in Politics* there are reprinted three
essays with Coleridge for their theme, the second
of which, beginning upon page 84, discusses him

by reference to Sir Hall Caine's *Life* and to certain
other commentators :

" The public (Patmore remarks) has little reason to trouble itself . . . whether the mistake that
he made in marrying Miss Fricker was not great
enough to justify an informal separation. . . .
Beyond the comparatively venial fault of making
an unsuitable marriage—and for him probably
any marriage would have been unsuitable—there
is extraordinarily little matter for moral censure
in the poet's history. He has never been sus-
pected of having broken the bond between himself and his wife by any immorality (p. 86).

" There was no fault on Coleridge's side in the
fact that latterly he and his wife found it convenient to dwell apart (p. 90) . . . and what
could the pair have done better than amicably
drop into the habit of paying independent visits
of indefinite duration to the houses of different
friends ? (p. 91).

" The fault was not in separating, but in having
come together (p. 95)."

That, then, was the attitude of Coventry Patmore to a typical hard case ; that was the *modus
vivendi* or compromise that his experience sub-
mitted to his philosophy. It differs clearly from
divorce in that it allows neither of the married pair
after separating to marry again. But it permits
them to separate. But why was it necessary that
they should have legally married at all ? This
question, which an increasing number of young

people seems to be asking, and answering in the negative, every year, is entitled to an answer from the poet who is, beyond question, the most subtle philosopher on marriage that the modern, western world has yet produced.

Coventry Patmore thought that the chief use of law and sanction, which are necessarily clumsy instruments when applied to any sacramental or symbolic uses, was to hold the lovers in check at the moment following their officially plighted troth.   It was to stand an external Witness over them at a critical corner, in order to remind them, at the inevitable moment of reaction when the heart like another Judas denies itself, that an act of faith which seems disappointed in the very letter of its bond can yet contain, for those who endure the trial of its probation, the fruits which they hoped to shake from the tree of life at a date when the seeds had hardly struck the lair in which they were designed to shoot the rod, the root, and finally the flower, of their secret being.

II. "A DAUGHTER OF COVENTRY PATMORE
(SISTER MARY CHRISTINA)"

This is a terrible book, in which the beautiful but tragic story of Emily Patmore, poet and nun, is briefly told.   The third child and eldest daughter of the poet, she was born in 1853, joined the Society of the Holy Child Jesus in 1873, and died of consumption, apparently brought on by her mor-

tifications, in 1882 at the age of twenty-nine. Her
character was heroic ; her soul that of a poet ; the
substance (and often the form) of her poetry as
authentic as any to be found, among the small section of Christian mystical verse, in English literature.   An immature daughter of the Muse, she
stands beside Emily Brontë and Christina Rossetti,
and above Emily Dickinson, both in her life and in
her verse. Her peculiar virtue was indeed a
combination of the qualities that we meet in her
namesakes, Emily and Christina.

But, though her biographer and introducer,
(being themselves Religious) lack the detachment
necessary to divine this, the evidence of her character, poetry, portraits, and the progress of her
spiritual life, including its ecstatic end, suggest
that she had not a religious vocation at all.   This
saying will seem less hard when we recall how
every influence, at home and at school (she was
educated at a convent), plus her father's and step-
mother's characters, conspired to turn, admittedly
at her own entreaty, a highly imaginative, passionate nature into conventual life.   By abetting these
influences, Emily accomplished the terrible task of
turning her own nature upside down and contort-
ing herself to fit the Procrustean bed whereon
circumstances, her obscure instincts, and the only
half reluctant zeal of others, combined to pen her.
The beautiful abortion that resulted, familiar in
parallel histories, needs no emphasis, but each
example, like each reading of a great tragedy,

seems to have a more ghastly loveliness than the
last.   The clue is discernible in this well-written
book, but it requires a detached and loving eye to
decipher it.   Observe : Emily chose this Society
because, being a teaching Order, its nuns live in
some contact with the world.   Her deepest instinct told her that such a life was more Christlike
than that of contemplative nuns ; but no one further reminded this ardent follower of her Master
that the example which He bequeathed, to heroic
souls, was one of a life in, but not of, this world.
The idea of Christ living in a monastery is felt by
all to be profane.   Emily could divine this, because she was of the heroic order herself.   But
had she ever heard any ask if conventual life be not
really for the less heroic, of both sexes ?   Acci-
dentally veil this inference from the heroic spirit
sometimes found in a born poet, and you produce
the artificial " vocation ' of Emily Patmore, every
subsequent step in which, to the death-bed vision
itself, becomes predictable.

Those who knew her regard her as an uncanon-
ized ' saint.'   The deeper and truer view is, I
think, one of an heroic genius contorted till it
assumes a form, intenser indeed but (strictly speaking) monstrous, because not that for which it was
intended by its Maker.   As things fell, there
remain a few fragments of lovely verse ; an in-
spiring example of misdirected genius, and no
more.   Emily Patmore's poems were contained
in a small note-book, and were first printed, I

think, in Mr. Basil Champney's Life of her father.
It is good, however, to meet some of them again,
or others for the first time, in this story of her own
life.   Future editions of the *Oxford Book of English
Mystical Verse* should certainly include examples.
As they are little known, it is a pleasure to quote
the following stanzas from two considerable
poems :

MY HOUR IS NOT YET COME

Thine hour, my Lord, I hear Thee say :
Desirable that hour must be
Which straitens, by its short delay,
The Ruler of Eternity.
Oh ! let me then in Thee rejoice,
And grant me such an hour to know !
 I hear Thy voice
Reply, in accents grave and low :
" Hora amantis illa est
Qua pro amico patitur."

   . . . .

O Love !   How blinded then are they
Who paint Thee crowned with roses bright !
'Tis well, indeed, for such to say
That Love is still bereft of sight.
But they who on the Truth do gaze,
As well as may be here below,
 Love thorny ways
Better than all the flowers that blow.
" Hora amantis illa est
Qua pro amico patitur."

LIFE AND DEATH

. . . .

When the youth whom Christ called to his college
First to bury his father had sped,
He was told by the Father's beloved
That the dead might bury their dead.
But the God of the ancients departed,
As His son again has said,
Lo! He is the God of the living,
He is not the God of the dead.
Then, dying, imprisoned spirit
Be patient beneath thy load,
For that which thou shalt inherit
Is Life—and the Life of God.

To Dom Anscar Vonier, who writes the preface, Emily suggests, metaphorically, " The Angel in the Cloister." She does ; but it is impossible to quell the still, small voice that whispers " she was intended for something else " : To live, and so to write, a *wife's* version of her father's epic theme, beginning at its married levels, and with a genius potentially, to say the least, not inferior to his own. The presence of a tragedy such as this makes praise or blame impertinent. The people nominally responsible, including Emily herself, not knowing of what they are witnesses, become like animalculae, too small to see, as the heroic spirit thus aborted hangs above them.

H

OSCAR BROWNING

THE death of Oscar Browning at the great age of eighty-six removed a famous ghost from public life, though a personality vivid enough, indeed, from the circle of his intimates and former pupils. It was his fate to outlive his generation, his successes, his failures, his reputation, and a sympathetic reader of his volume of later Memories could not but respond to the courage and cheerfulness with which he disguised the loneliness and isolation of his last decade. He stalked in exile, though by choice, in the Eternal City, where he had lived since his departure from King's College, Cambridge, more than twelve years before, and seemed but the latest addition to its historic monuments. For he was a great personality who somehow failed to become a great man, and, as a teacher, a friend, a man of the world, was, above all, a quickening influence in the lives of others. Eton, where he was for fifteen years a master ; Cambridge where he was for thirty-three years a don, were ideal fields for his activities, and it seems tragic, yet symbolic, that he should have lived so full a life, and reached such an advanced age, without having been elected Provost of either college. Ideally, at least, he ought to have succeeded Austen Leigh as Provost of King's, and whatever other gifts Leigh's successors have brought to that foundation, none could have rivalled Oscar Browning in the gesture with which he would have presided. He would have endowed the headship of the college with a personality, and looked as worthy as Dr. Johnson of his part.

One falls naturally into the eighteenth-century cadence when writing of him, for O. B. was by temperament, by sympathy, we might almost be allowed to say by the date of his birth, an eighteenth-century figure. In him its ideal of the scholar, the statesman in little, and the man of the world, was combined. That he should be remembered, as perhaps he will be remembered, as the greatest Cambridge don of the latter half of the nineteenth century, seems an anti-climax, such was the spell of his personality on all capable of penetrating beyond its surface of egoism, and its whimsical adulation of the great. The obituary notices were little more than a tissue of anecdotes in illustration of his characteristic weakness, and left the impression of a celebrated butt, whose reputation depended upon amiable follies. But such an impression would be unjust. There was more than buffoonery in Oscar Browning, and it is in the hope of correcting, without contradicting, the prevailing legend, that the present writer ventures, as an old pupil, to record the impressions left by intercourse with Oscar Browning in the years 1903–7 at Cambridge. The O. B. at that time was not only Senior Fellow of King's College, but Historical Tutor, and all members of the college who entered for the Historical Tripos came first under his tuition.

He was one of the few dons who were generally known outside academic circles, and his personality was already a legend.   It was therefore with a mixture of curiosity and awe that the freshman first entered the rooms that were to become so familiar.   The legend is condensed in the couplet which every one remembers :

> Two things there be men cannot flee :
> Death, and a friendship with O.B.

The freshman was led to expect a colossal egoist, surrounded by Arundel prints and framed telegrams from Royalties, the centre of a half-humorous splendour, a kind of privileged Punchinello among dons.   His huge head and massive features, his linèd and sallow face, on which experience seemed to have stamped itself in fire and smoke, were sufficiently impressive, and crowned a short, bulky figure set upon stumpy legs that disappeared into a huge pair of square black boots.   It is a mistake to suppose that short people necessarily lack presence, and the touch of the grotesque in his gait only made one more alive to his force and vitality. This terrific physiognomy was lit by a queer smile that seemed to shine through a smoky cloud, and preluded a hearty and effusive welcome. He rolled about like a playful bear, and hugged instead of shaking hands with his visitor.

His rooms were lined with books and pictures, and the wall-paper of white and gold, the prints, the framed telegrams were all that one had been led to expect. He did most of the talking, and that was often about himself. His talk was like a flow of molten lava that bore every kind of reminiscence on its tide ; an incredible medley, sometimes astonishing in the extent of its unconscious humour, sometimes witty and informing ; sometimes prolix and tending apparently nowhither. In the course of its flow the freshman's affairs seemed to be obliterated till it would pause as unaccountably as it had begun, and the object of one's visit would be discussed. Then it became plain that the course of reading to be pursued, the lectures to be attended, were only incidents of the tuition that the pupil was to receive—ingredients necessary, no doubt, but subordinate to the much wider process of forming an educated man of the world. The pupil was to be launched upon the sea of university life, because that provided the varied means for following his own tastes and developing his own temperament. One was asked to his Sunday At Homes to listen to classical music, and enrolled a member of the Political Society which met every Monday in his rooms, when a paper was read, a discussion held, and a

vote taken on the subject of the debate.   This
often wandered amusingly far from the subject of
the paper.

Most pupils had the opportunity of joining this
society, which the O. B. had founded in 1876.
Among members afterwards famous were J. K.
Stephen, Mr. G. M. Trevelyan, Mr. Lowes
Dickinson, Mr. Austen Chamberlain, and many
others.   That there might be no backsliding, each
member had to read a paper in turn ; the order
was decided by lot.   When we assembled, the
president always being in evening dress, with a
crimson silk handkerchief tucked into the left-
hand corner of his waistcoat, he advanced toward
us with a little bag from which every one drew a
number.   This determined the order 'in which
we were to speak.   The president himself was
never allowed to address us out of his turn, and
was accustomed to make up in length for the
shortness of any other speeches.   This plan of
drawing numbers set all the young men upon
their legs, and that they might learn to speak
properly, each in turn had to address the society
from the hearth-rug.

So soon as the reader had began to recite from
his manuscript, the president would draw his
crimson handkerchief from its corner, lean back
in his chair, and completely over his head with it.
The handkerchief was not removed until the
reading of the paper had been finished.   The
combined formality and humour of these evenings

robbed them of the unreal solemnity that often
attends youthful debating societies, nor was anything more remarkable in Mr. Browning himself
than the way in which he invested everything he
did with an air of individuality.

There were generally good reasons for his
apparently eccentric actions.   He was the last
don, I think, to dress every night for hall, and
when asked whether this was because he was an
upholder of tradition, he replied : " If the dons
do not dress for hall they will get a bad dinner.
How can they expect the kitchen to take a pride
in its cooking, if they themselves show no respect
for the kitchen at their public meals ? "   He
always sent out formal invitations to his luncheons,
dinners, and At Homes, carefully expressed in the
third person ; and there was no doubt that he did
so to teach, or to remind, the undergraduates of a
formality which, whether ordinarily used or not,
was part of a general social training that they
ought to carry away from the university.   It was
in numberless little ways, of which the above are
trifling examples, that Oscar Browning was an
educative influence.   He represented a standard
of behaviour, a manner of life, that his eccen-
tricities only emphasized.   In contact with him
young men escaped from the atmosphere of pro-
vinciality, and in him the spirit of an uncom-
mercial society, in which manners, leisure, sport,
art, scholarship, were equally important, seemed
to be embodied.   He had the priceless gift of

personality, and contrived to suggest a society of such people, and to lift the idea of education beyond any narrowly academic spheres.

Like the great Lord Chesterfield, whose *Letters* are worth all the treatises on education ever written, Oscar Browning was a born master of novices.   It is for this that he deserves to be remembered, and the best, perhaps the only, memorial of his gift would be a collection of papers from his pupils recording how he had coloured their imaginations and quickened their lives.   To his pupils he was generous and stimulating.   If his lectures were jokes, they reminded one that the object of lectures should be not to provide notes that would enable one to satisfy examiners, but to stimulate interest and excite to private study ; if his books could not be taken seriously, his influence was none the less useful and fecundating.   His idea was to stimulate each pupil's own gifts, to widen the range of his interests, and to produce not first-class honours, or a man with a degree, but a personality for whom both men of culture and men of action would feel respect.

King's College, he said, existed " for the manu-facture of statesmen," and we learnt to read, to speak, to debate, and to study the arts, with an eye beyond University prizes.   How rare such an aim is in any schoolmaster or don, needs no saying. It is rare not because it is fine in itself, but because only a fine personality can make it effective.   So, he took the provincially minded pupil to travel with him ; the boor was civilized at his parties ; the scholar at Newmarket ; the " rugger rough " at Bach concerts in his tutor's rooms. These ideals radiated from his belief in the History School of King's, but, no doubt because he had been fourth classic himself, he never fully realized that history is an imperfect educational study because it lacks that essential substratum of grit which grammar gives to Greek and Latin, and addition and subtraction to mathematics. The learning of these is a true discipline. You either know them or not, and cannot disguise your limitations. But who " knows " history, or can know it ? It was their history tutor, not the historical tripos, that educated Oscar Browning's pupils.

His ashes, by his own wish, rest in the college chapel, and his spirit will haunt the foundation in the reconstruction of which he played a part not too generously rewarded. His memory will endure as a legend, but behind the legend was a born educator whose influence was the more valuable in that it was devoted less to theory than to example, and was concerned with much more than the gaining of degrees and the contents of books.

1923.

THE POEMS OF ALICE MEYNELL

THE substance of most books of modern verse
is the scattered emotions remaining to
those who have no philosophy of life, who cannot
see the wood for the trees, who suffer the ache of
an inner vacuity, who clutch at the passing straw
of any transient emotion because that wandering
wisp is the only tangible thing in the disorder of
their attention.   But an ache for something which
is not there, a confession of something wanting, a
search for some centre on which to repose : none
of these is a substitute for a positive quality.   It
is the absence of a personality which these reveal ;
they are symptoms, not revelations.   The lack
which earnestness, striving, purpose (ugly words
for ugly vices) betray in life and in prose, this
scatter-brained emotionalism betrays in poetry.
The first cannot speak, nor the second sing.   This
explains why we read most contemporary books of
verse with impatience, and why, if we read many
of them, a sense of standard seems to depart from
us.

Here I have tried to make the effort which
most readers will hardly be at pains to make for

themselves, the effort to diagnose the disorder of which much modern verse is the reflection.   Since this dis-ease, with the disillusion which accompanies it, is now endemic, we should fortify ourselves by a study of those writers, classical and modern, who in different degrees belong to the true order of poetry.   This order is to be recognized by its affirmative note and by the unmistakable presence of attention.   Now full attention will be awakened only by recognition of some reality.   It will have a centre of gravity, however small, from which, as from the sun or from the daisy, rays of light will spread to the joy of every eye once focused upon it.   For the poet is always the seer ; and though we boast that he merely expresses that which we already know, he gives us, in truth, his eyes for a moment, his eyes as well as that whereon they have rested.   The multitude of books of modern verse, then, is a triumph not of inspiration but of bookishness.   The faster the number grows the more important does it become to return to the standard set by the few, the true poets among them.   Mrs. Meynell, like Mr. W. H. Davies, had to bear her share of the common burden, and submit without undue dismay to many appreciations of herself.

The reception of her work was somewhat curious.   The early volume was well received by those whose praise was worth having.   Then she turned to prose, and that was also praised, mainly, I think, by the rank and file of critics, except Pat-

more, who preferred the prose to the verse !
What did she think of his preference ?   It is
hard for a writer who began with verse, and whose
verse was applauded, to find her prose preferred
thereto ; the harder the greater the critic.   I can
fancy that Mrs. Meynell weighed his words more
than those of others, and that her response must
have been, not " It is unfair to say that," but
simply " Is it true ? "   Since she returned to
verse, she must on reflection have said to herself :
" A writer has two media.   He need not limit
himself to one.   To seek to limit himself in
accordance with the verdict of others would be to
surrender to the critics who are far too apt to
interfere.   I shall write a poem, gentlemen, when
the mood is upon me, and an essay when I will."
At this point in her reflections the drawing-room
door was opened, and a ghostly line of critics
took their leave.

   It is possible that the preference has changed
since then.   For myself I am on the side of the
verses, because they are free from a quality which
sometimes may be discerned in the prose, the
quality (how far is it a quality ?) of preciousness.
The only prose to which this essay must refer is
that provided by the titles.   Anyone acquainted
with the essays would recognize the author of a
poem called " Renouncement," and the author of
another poem entitled " The Lover Urges The
Better Thrift."   Let us pause upon these titles
for a moment.   Though there is precedent for

the old word renouncement, few contemporary Englishmen would use it until they had first thought of, and then rejected, renunciation.   It is not idiomatic.   It is correct, but a trifle too conscious of its correctness.   It attracts our notice to itself.   Why was it preferred to renunciation ?   I often asked myself the question, for this title long discouraged me from reading further.   The answer is interesting.   It came to the pen of the writer before the word renunciation and not afterward ;   and it came before because a long residence in France had made the French form of a word more habitual than the English, which flowered upon her page in a landscape of French memories. A similar explanation should be remembered in regard to the essays, but I doubt how far it would affect most of the instances on which a critic would fasten.   " The Lover Urges The Better Thrift " is a good instance, because either the reader feels a certain euphuistic quality in these words, or he does not.   Those who feel it can say only that it is not a title which Shakespeare would have chosen, or Wordsworth, the great master of idiom, or even Browning, who was ever ready to make the language dance to any, except an euphuistic, tune.   Meredith might have used it ;   but with him we desert our English idiom to indulge in a scholar's escapade.   Like Carlyle, he improvised upon the language ;   he never let it play its native tune.   The result was a series of effects ;   but these were dearly purchased by the corruption of

the language, which encouraged its further corruption in others.   Preciousness, taken seriously,
has been defined to be the learned corruption of
language, which it teases into odd shapes and
treats to affectations.   Let the reader ask himself
whether " The Lover Urges The Better Thrift "
is not a departure from the ease of English
idiom.

It is just that " Renouncement " became to
weariness Mrs. Meynell's famous poem: the one
poem which will always be quoted from her.   No
one will ever ask what she wrote.   She was the
author of " Renouncement."   To be identified
with one work, in this sense, is to have attained
the certainty of reputation.   It is the most simple
test, and the best.   To revive the freshness of this
familiar piece, let us note first that it is a sonnet,
and secondly how it grew under her hand.   The
sonnet is properly the favourite form of the smaller
poets.   It is the favourite form because it is the
shortest metrical scheme yet acclimatized to
English prosody.   While the great poets, like
Wordsworth, have been the greatest masters of
the sonnet, the poets of the second rank, like
Rossetti, have done well, even excellently, in this
form.   Its narrowness is a quality, not a defect,
and like a Scotch burn, it is properly the haunt of
the grayling and the minnows.   Blanco White
lives as the author of one sonnet, Davenant as
the author of one song.   Mrs. Meynell lives
chiefly as the author of another, around which her

other poems still cluster like facets round the table of a gem.   Her quality is a perfection of integrity which needs a small compass to display itself.   Thus " Renouncement " suggests her range and is an instance of its quality.   To observe this, note, secondly, the improvements made in the final version.   " Love " has been changed to " thought " in the second and third lines, an obvious gain in directness and perspicuity ; and " dearest " has become " sweetest " in the fourth line.   This last change has involved another : the substitution of " fairest " for " sweetest " in line five.   These varium readings may be excused because they give a new interest, as the changes have given a richer content, to a poem by now in danger of being too familiar to the reader.   Let me note one other change which is also an improvement.   " The Lady of the Lambs " has become " The Shepherdess." Wordsworth would have liked the later title better.

Having inferred the compass of Mrs. Meynell's work from the fact that her famous piece is a sonnet, we shall know for what to hope, and for what not to look, in her work generally.   A small compass implies intensity, and intensity, together with a small compass, implies an absence of vitality in the larger sense.   If we turn to the drawing by Sargent which adorns the volume of *Collected Poems*, what do we see ?   We see a tall, slender figure, the stem, as it were, of a delicate, refined face, a face a little weary, as if it weɪe masked with the ashes of a fire which had wasted the spirit within. The distinction, the beauty is apparent, but there is the sense, often to be observed in an aristocratic face, of the end, of the weariness of a long road, most of which lies behind the traveller. The thread which binds the sheaf of Mrs. Meynell's verses is a thread of sadness. Renunciation, we perceive, is the characteristic subject, for her mind is preoccupied with tragic moments, moments bravely borne no doubt, but requiring bravery to bear them. Life is a burden to this poetess, not a joy. It imposes too great a strain upon her nerves. She has to brace herself to live, and is less conscious of life than of the daily price to be paid for living. In a poem entitled "The Modern Mother," the mother hopes not for the love of her son but for his "forgiveness." Had she not bestowed upon him the tragic present of life ? Again, in "Parentage," a poem written before the War, we are told that women who bear children are the real slayers, because war and disease prey upon living things and everything which is born is led to the slaughter. The experiences which move her most, and the poignancy of which she uses all the resources of her art to prevent us from losing, are tragic, cruel moments ; and these she contemplates with the fascination of a magnet to its pole. An exquisite example of her talent in this kind is "Maternity" :

> One wept whose only child was dead,
>   New-born, ten years ago.
> " Weep not ; he is in bliss," they said.
>   She answered, " even so.
>
> Ten years ago was born in pain
>   A child, not now forlorn.
> But oh, ten years ago, in vain,
>   A mother, a mother was born."

An acid touches every poem as with a cautery.
Let us note a few touches which are the more
revealing because they are touches only, shadows
which steal upon her work like the twilight, little
clouds which come between her spirit and the
sun. In " Veni Creator " she asks, not if there
is one Joy unknown to God, but if there is one
" lowliness " unknown to Him, and cries :

> Look at the mournful world Thou hast decreed,

and at the " hapless " men who know their " hap-
lessness " within it. These adjectives coming
spontaneously to her pen haunt her poems from
the beginning. In " Why wilt Thou Chide ? "
the attainment is " to be denied " some one ; and
the rejected lover is told that no one can dare to
" hope " for a part in his " despair." In " San
Lorenzo's Mother," a poem deservedly admired,
the last verse runs as follows :

> There is One alone who cannot change ;
> Dreams are we, shadows, visions strange ;
>   And all I give is given to One.
> I might mistake my dearest son,
>   But never the Son who cannot change.

I

The conviction which burns at the heart of this faith must not blind our eyes : the emphasis of the last two lines is distributed equally between them. If the emphasis was not so strong upon line four, the fifth line would be much weakened. Therefore we are conscious not only of the faith but of the tragic admission which has made this faith unfaltering. Again, in the charming poem, " An Unmarked Festival," which celebrates the first chance meeting of two lovers, Mrs. Meynell was interested not only in the great evẹnt which came suddenly upon them, but that it went as it came for long unmarked. In " The Unexpected Peril " she is more explicit. Her youth, she says, was never " abounding " nor

> In love with the sufficient day.

Her " first slumber nightly rehearsed " her " last." She goes still further :

> My shroud was in the flocks ; the hill
>   Within its quarry locked my stone ;
> My bier grew in the woods ; and still
>   Life spurred me where I paused alone.

When the siege of her spirit was raised a little later, her new house-mate, " ease," filled her with hardly less misgiving, and in the end she implores the Angels of Labour and Pain, for it is " fear " which can best teach her.

The latest volume, *A Father of Women*, abounded in similar touches. In a poem upon

the Lord's Prayer heaven is " unconceivable."
The Thy Will is " inexorable yet implored " ;
the divine words are charged with an " unknown
purpose." With a sense almost perverse she
declares in the " The Two Questions " that her
mind is appalled not by the sufferings of the innocent heart, but by the punishment of the wicked :
a point of view which (unless I misinterpret) is
seeking for some subtlety of suffering where a
healthy vitality would find joy. The most joyful of English poets, Thomas Traherne, the
exquisite Anglican mystic, whose subject was
always felicity, and Coventry Patmore, the most
masculine of poets, are alike at least in this that
both of them number among the joys of heaven
the spectacle of thoroughly bad people receiving
their deserts. But Mrs. Meynell would exchange
that masculine joy for some ache of pity or desire:
without an edge she would hardly recognize her
felicity. " The Divine Privilege " is " to be
alone the sacrificed." In " The Treasure " life is

> How weak,
> How sad, how brief! O how divine, divine !

Indeed it is hardly too much to say that her
imagination was only awakened fully by the
spectacle of suffering, and when she sings it is in
elegy. " The Letter of a Girl to her own Old
Age," with its long line of lamentation and the
skilful droop of the feminine endings, is characteristic ; and yet, if the spectacle of suffering were

offered to her in its nakedness, as Mestrovic
offered it to us all in his " Crucifixion," I fancy
that she would turn away her eyes and declare that
it was not bearable.   Such a turning away I
should regard as evidence of the truth of this
criticism.   We do turn away when we see ourselves face to face.   Consequently Mrs. Meynell
must place herself slightly at an oblique angle,
and view the moments which possess her mind a
little from one side.   She shoots beside the mark
rather than at it ; and her arrows, like the bright
glances of the robin, fly the straighter because they
seem to spy their object from one side.   This
gave a bird-like quality to her writing, which is
at once intense but detached.

We gain from her work, then, this : not, at
first, an extension of our humanity but an added
sharpness to our consciousness.   But in so far as
this consciousness is concerned with experiences
not peculiar in themselves, but common to all
men, it is enriching.   The experience of Strephon
in " St. Catharine of Siena " is an experience of
mankind ; Catharine herself is feminine humanity.   Hackneyed or official themes are trans-
formed by this insight.   Shakespeare's Tercen-
tenaries became two dates in Mrs. Meynell's own
life, and the death of Edith Cavell is seen as perhaps Edith herself saw it : a nurse who watched
at her own death-bed, a woman who quietly
waited for the dawn.   We penetrate beyond the
heroine of the copy-book to the natural woman,

and go with her to her execution. This is the quality which raises Mrs. Meynell's verse to the highest point possible to its own order. Each poem, too, is carefully reasoned, and the reader who does not follow the argument will miss the whole ; for intellectually no less than emotionally the verse has point. This intellectual concentration is a dangerous quality. " Via et Veritas et Vita " is an epigram, but a good one. " Veni Creator " and " Why wilt Thou Chide ? " seem, or seem near to, intellectual conceits. The latter poem apparently offers an impossibly subtle consolation. Renunciation, consolation—how the theme recurs !

The limits of this poetry are sharply defined, and the substance is the clearer for them. That substance is true and genuine, but it is not gay or great. Joy is a quality of strength, and only in the great poets is intensity wholly free from tensity. The edge of a refined intelligence which we carry away from our reading has been gained by a tension of the nerves, which are robbed of some of their tone by the strain imposed upon them. We cannot repose upon this poetry. It is a tonic rather than a wine. It is life at its most intense, rather than at its highest, which we find here. For life at its highest is pure joy ; at the centre of joy there is peace ; and genius is too simple to be unhappy.

But that I may not seem to have bent the quotations to my argument or to have cast a precon-

ceived shadow upon them, let me conclude with
one quotation which shows her imagination at
large and free.   It comes from " Christ in the
Universe " ; and the subject of the poem is His
dealing with other worlds than the earth :

> Nor, in our little day,
> May His devices with the heavens be guessed,
> His pilgrimage to thread the Milky Way
> Or His bestowals there be manifest.
>
> But in the eternities,
> Doubtless we shall compare together, hear
> A million alien Gospels, in what guise
> He trod the Pleiades, the Lyre, the Bear.
>
> O, be prepared, my soul !
> To read the inconceivable, to scan
> The million forms of God those stars unroll
> When, in our turn, we show to them a Man.

That has a vitality, a splendour comparable to
some of Francis Thompson's imagery : the lattice-
window has been opened ; we feel the breath of
the sky.   The air comes finely in on the thought
here expressed.   But we may not remain long at
the open window, and are led by Mrs. Meynell to
explore the shadowy interior of Humanity's
familiar house.

SHELLEY THE DRAMATIST

H IS centenary celebrations were robbed of
unreality on the afternoon of November
13, 1922, when the first public performance of
The Cenci was given. It was a great occasion, for until that afternoon there had been no
opportunity for a considered judgment. Not
only was this the first public performance, but
only the second that had occurred. The first
took place on May 7, 1886, when the Shelley
Society had presented it on the stage before two
thousand four hundred members, each of whom
had paid a guinea for his seat. Those who
witnessed both performances must have been
very few, but at length the one honour lacking
to the poet was paid, and the one service that he
could render to us was fittingly acknowledged.

The play stands apart from others in the
present writer's recollection in that he has never
been able to open it, at any place, or to read any
line in any scene, without feeling compelled half
against his will to read the drama through from
cover to cover. Though he knew much of it
by heart, the performance proved a revelation.

The *annus mirabilis* of Shelley's life has been
called 1819, because both *Prometheus Unbound*
and *The Cenci* were composed in this year.   In
his excellent essay on the poet, Mr. Arthur
Symons says :
   " When we come to what Browning calls ' the
unrivalled Cenci,' we are in another atmosphere,
and in this atmosphere, not his own, he walks
with equal certainty. . . .   In the dedication, he
distinguishes it from his earlier works, ' visions
which impersonate my own apprehension of the
beautiful and the just.' . . .   *The Cenci* is the
greatest play written in English since *The Duchess
of Malfi.* . . .   He has solved the problem of
the poem [and of the play in blank verse] which
shall be conventional speech and yet pure poetry.
. . .   It was probably more difficult for him to
do than to write *Prometheus Unbound*.   He went
straight from one to the other, and was probably
unconscious quite how much he had done."
   This passage (I am not sure how far in Mr.
Symons' intention) points to the usually neglected
connection of the *Prometheus* with *The Cenci*.   The
two are complementary ; they interpret one
another ; neither can be fully understood apart.
   Even when we read *The Cenci*, we feel its chief
defect to be the incredible devilry of the Count,
in whom there is no human feeling, no humanity
at all.   A being who adds no other superhuman
qualities to superhuman fiendishness revolts not
the conscience only but probability, and is there-

fore dramatically weak. It is not enough to reply that the Renaissance appears to have produced such monsters. The closer we come to them the greater is the difficulty of presenting them in art ; but, when reading the play, we are tempted to suppose that an actor might humanize the part by the simple process of impersonating it. The test was disappointing. A devil must act Count Cenci if he is to be acted credibly. It was nevertheless admitted that the play " improved " toward the end, and the explanation is worth recording. In the first half of the drama the Count dominates every instant of it. In the second, after he has been murdered, his remorselessness is replaced by the engine of the law, which becomes the antagonist of Beatrice. The heroism of Marzio enables the play to rise from horror to tragedy, and humanity returns. This is the reason why the later acts were preferred to the earlier, and why in them the actors' tasks ceased to be impossible. We share indeed the feeling of Beatrice that the spirit of her dead father still dominates the action, but this spirit becomes credible when it is no longer incarnate in the body of one man but in the System of law or government. We have no experience of a human devil, but the implacable machinery of an institution we have all witnessed at one time or another, and thus in the later acts our imagination ceases to be strained. The transformation comes so late, however, that judgment is already im-

pounded, and the play is dismissed as an inspired
abortion.

In suggesting that this judgment is too hasty,
I submit that Shelley was instinctively acting on
the Greek model, and that, in the year during
which these two plays were composed, he had at
the back of his mind a vision of the Greek trilogy.
Prometheus Unbound is a lyrical drama, and *The
Cenci* a tragedy supposed to be based upon historic
facts.   The conflict of the earlier is a conflict of
the spirit ; the characters are drawn from myth
and partake of divine or superhuman nature.
The conflict in *The Cenci* takes place in the world
of fact ; the characters, with one exception, are
human, the scene historic.   With these considerations in mind, and remembering that the planes
and consequently the conditions of the two
dramas are different, it becomes apparent that
the conflict with which both deal is the same
conflict, and that the antagonists are identical in
both.   There is therefore less reason for surprise
that the writing of the one immediately followed
that of the other.   If the presumed trilogy had
been completed, the interconnection of its two first
members would have been apparent before now.

Briefly, the part of Prometheus in the lyrical
drama is that of Beatrice in the tragedy, and the
personality of Jove is repeated in that of the
Count.   Why, then, is Jove acceptable and Cenci
repudiated by the imagination of the reader ?
We accept the tyrant of the myth because he is

confessedly a fiend, whereas an entirely fiendish man is unbelievable. Jove is the dramatic projection of universal or at least religious forces ; the Count embodies social or collective agency, either of which a single person overtly challenges in vain. The clue to the conception of the Count is the terrible, yet familiar, fact that the collective action of human beings, in the systems and institutions that are necessary to their existence, often acts so diabolically that its human officers are appalled at what is being done, though, being severally but cogs on a wheel not of their own contriving, their immediate duty blinds their consciences to the real nature of the proceedings. A man of genius is not usually a cog on the wheel of any human machinery, and when his genius is " a nerve " as sensitive as Shelley's these impersonal processes are recorded vividly. If this sensitiveness is accompanied, as Shelley's was, by a conscience, it concentrates through the burning-glass of his imagination on the evil that escapes the eyes of lesser men. Indeed, from the horror of this impersonal evil no man, once awakened to it, can escape.

This, the real social evil, is the theme of *The Cenci*. No human being in his personal activities is as cruel as the Count, but we all consent to abominations no less frightful in our social ones. The Count's cold implacability is exactly mirrored in the machinery by which law and order are maintained. Sooner or later we discover that infernal wickedness is only too familiar in the everyday workings of the institutions that we are brought up to respect and obey, since the truth is that these agencies fall below the moral standard of humanity at least as often as they rise above it. The very power necessary to maintain their usefulness endows them with a force for evil that finds no parallel elsewhere in human experience. Our cherished institutions are fully equipped for horrors, and only a vigilant conscience can save us from them. Revolutions are created not by agitators but by reactionary governments, and the way of Beatrice is the way of all courageous souls whose consciences have been outraged beyond endurance by their fathers and masters.

This is the truism that the two dramas project on their several planes. In *Prometheus Unbound* we see the embodiment of the superstitions that claim man's obedience in the name of all the popular idolatries. Prometheus is the hero in man who, recognizing the superstition for what it is, becomes thereby possessed of a secret which shall dethrone the phantom when once the hero's knowledge is common property. He refuses to yield this knowledge by obeisance to Jove, who chains him in torment to the rock. Superstition is incapable of perceiving that its impermanence resides in itself, and cannot be prevented by persecution. Against the silent steps of Time nothing permanently prevails. Thus Prometheus is shown enduring till the Car of the Hour arrives, when Demogorgon or Eternity, describing himself as Jove's own child, descends and leads him to the abyss.

This drama, which is in perpetual process of enactment in the sphere of religious and scientific orthodoxy, has its counterpart in the growth of human institutions. The former is best presented in a myth : the latter in a history. But no social mechanism is self-conscious, and thus there is an inevitable failure of illusion when its action, to be made self-conscious, is presented through the deeds and words of one man. Industrialism may grind human lives to powder ; the prison system may be more implacable than any of its officers ; a Trust may crush the small competitor by a remorseless conspiracy that no private individuals would countenance, but neither Business, nor Law, nor the Prison Commission avows in words the cruel unfaith which inspires them or advocates the moral theory to which their acts conform. Each of these is a machine and has no conscience save in the persons of its officers, and these are generally too much absorbed in their routine to suspect where the machine and their conscience must conflict. Thus our toleration of collective action is usually as complete as our horror when once the rationale of its action is put into words.

The action of all these systems has driven many victims to despair or suicide, and their relation to individuals is such that any human being who opposes them directly almost inevitably converts his defeat into a crime. His despair is intensified because his oppressor is intangible. A corporation is very difficult to kick. A victim can touch it only in the persons of its officers ; and it is the last disillusion of a tortured soul to find that his endeavour to oppose a Trust has landed him in gaol on the misrepresentative charge of assaulting a policeman. At this point he feels deserted by God and man because his own conscience can accept neither passive defeat nor the justice of a verdict which condemns him by a distinction between the system and its officers, when this distinction is to his disadvantage, but refuses to make it when the Trust is the aggressor. This impersonal Thing can do no wrong to him, apparently ; the law is its servant, if not part of itself ; but the moment he endeavours to defend himself against it by the smallest personal action, he is immediately charged with an assault—on some one else ! The Father of Lies could hardly devise a more perfect piece of irony.

One of the functions of art is to quicken our sympathies, for, as Shelley says : " until the mind can love, and admire, and trust, and hope, and endure, reasoned principles of moral conduct are seeds cast upon the highway of life which the unconscious passenger tramples into dust, although they would bear the harvest of his happiness." The appeal of beauty is to love at first sight, and this remains the poet's main concern, but the critic's function includes the definition of the obscurer sympathies that the poet awakens. The Count's aims, when translated into the sphere which they really dominate, are very revealing. His object was to " entrap the loathing will " of his victim, and Beatrice became convinced that her crime would be in allowing him to live.   She seemed so placed that the murder of her father was the only means of self-defence she had.

Before turning to Shelley's view of her dilemma let us glance at the behaviour of Prometheus in the like predicament.   Being a demi-god, and therefore like his antagonist immortal, he endures to the end, and he wins his victory by refraining from opposition, not by indulging it.   Thus, in the sense in which we human beings understand the term, neither the instinct for self-defence nor the impulse to murder could possess him.   Prometheus was superior to mortality in so much, could his example be of value to mortals ?

Shelley declares : " Revenge, retaliation, atonement, are pernicious mistakes.   If Beatrice had thought in this way, she would have been wiser and better, but she would never have been a tragic character."   Yet Marzio is made to assert " a keener pang has wrung a higher truth from my last breath.   She is most innocent."   Which is right ?   In the play, moreover, the murder has hardly been committed, when, by a dramatic coincidence, the Papal legate arrives to summon the Count to answer grave charges. The relief comes at the moment when it is too late to be of use, and thus helps to create the tragedy. We see, then, that Shelley demanded the same conduct from humanity as had been recorded of the demi-god. The dramatic coincidence in the tragedy plays the part of Demogorgon in the drama. The catastrophe is produced by its means. Fate, in each play, seems to be responsible. It has been said that no such person as Demogorgon exists. In the present tense this is true. He is the substance of things hoped for, and no more immediately real than any other aspiration. Faith, however, is a force not to be denied, for there is no courage without it. It is represented in both plays, and Shelley wished us to share his own allegiance to it.

At this point, let us appeal for illustration to the text. After her father's death, Beatrice finds the Law no less implacable than he, and she comes to identify his spirit with it. This identification, I have suggested, is not fanciful. When Cardinal Camillo tells her that a reprieve has been refused, he says suggestively :

> The Pope is stern ; not to be moved or bent.
> He looked as calm and keen as is the *engine*
> Which tortures and which kills, exempt itself
> From aught that it inflicts ; a marble form,
> A *rite*, a *law*, a *custom* : not a man.
> He frowned, as if to frown had been the trick
> Of his *machinery*.

This awakens in Beatrice precisely the mood produced in a victim of social machinery. She speaks of " an atmosphere," as if her father's spirit lived " in all that breathe." The crisis passes, but at the price of perfect disillusion, as negative of doubt as of faith, of despair as of hope. She confronts reality, and nothing remains. All barriers between her and It have crumbled. Its power and her will are equally matched. The result is a deadlock, for the intensity of the effort produces an effect of repose. Beyond this human imagination faints. It has touched the sky-line of mortality, and can no more. To misconceive this moment is to fall below it, as her mother does. Her clutches at the vinegar and hyssop are to Beatrice a belittlement of the thirst. Her farewell words reassert her instinctive self-justification in the manner of many victims of the State, the Law, the Army, on the barricade or the scaffold. The person of the Count, who is the symbol of these institutions, brings to light certain of their qualities which most people would miss, and this sufficiently excuses the sacrifice of immediate illusion that his presentment entails. Dramatic literature would be impoverished if Shelley had refused to invite defeat by shirking the initial difficulty. As it is, the unforgettable warning remains that human institutions become Molochs when we worship them, and like Molochs then devour their own children. *The Cenci* dramatizes this

K

moment on the institutional plane as *Prometheus Unbound* had done upon the intellectual. *The Cenci* is therefore much the more disturbing play, and would probably never have been permitted on the stage at all if its purport were generally understood. The thought that Shelley intended *The Cenci* to leave with us is to be found at the end of *Promethus Unbound* :

> To suffer woes which Hope thinks infinite ;
> To forgive wrongs darker than death or night ;
>   To defy Power, which seems omnipotent ;
> To love and bear ; to hope till Hope creates
> From its own wreck the thing it contemplates ;
>   Neither, to change, nor flatter, nor repent ;
> This, like thy glory, Titan, is to be
> Good, great and joyous, beautiful and free ;
> This is alone Life, Joy, Empire, and Victory.

Beatrice did " defy " her father, but the distinction between defiance and retaliation is subtle in the moment of action, and Beatrice failed to make it.   Count Cenci, once recognized for the antagonist he really is, becomes rather a fatherland than a father, and such human abstractions commit at times atrocities on their children for which incest is almost a literal description. To penetrate to this criticism of human institutions is to become aware of a horror which we cannot deny but dare not admit to be true.

If Shelley was instinctively working on the model of the Greek trilogy, but left only the first

two plays on nis central theme composed, we
cannot resist wondering in what form the third
and last would have projected it.   Such specu-
lation is not idle if it forces us to inquire what
aspect of the great conflict remained to be treated.
It is the essence of such subjects to provide in-
exhaustible motives for art, and the superstitious
idolatry that Shelley has exposed is not confined
to spiritual beliefs or to public machinery.

THE ART OF MR. CHAPLIN

A N American producer of films has lately offered to establish and endow a Chair of Cinema Research at one of the eight principal universities of his country. His object was to attract better talent to an industry the rewards of which are already enormous. How pathetic is the belief in the power of money ; how ineradicable the faith in professors ! All the previous art in the world has sprung from illiterate and unsophisticated people. Our art schools produce mainly teachers, and nothing is more risky to artistic aptitude than education. It is wiser, then, not to look to academies when we are considering the possibilities of the youngest of the arts. A more fruitful study is the practice of Mr. Charles Chaplin, an artist who has already given to the world the best that his vast public would allow. It is not necessary to examine all the work that he has done. It is sufficient to glance at one of his familiar masterpieces, and to prepare the way by admitting that at the moment he is meeting with the fate that attends all artists who have won their reputation but, necessarily, lost

their novelty.   The only infinite capacity of mankind is for ingratitude.

This admitted, we may then discriminate
between his works, and allow that *The Gold Rush*
is not the measure of his genius.   There is no
unity of idea in his latest film-play.   It has only
his physiognomy to hold it together, and such
story as there is is not a theme for the eye, a film-
story, but a succession of incidents in no organic
relation, incidents that might have been presented
in any form.   For once, the screen has not determined it, and for this reason *The Gold Rush* is not
true to the art of Mr. Chaplin.

In his chosen medium of the film, and in its
native province, the broader comedy (the film has
hardly won the fairy touch of pathos yet) Mr.
Chaplin is great.   Some maturer critics, who
suffer from an inverted fear of sameness that
novelty itself cannot assuage, qualified their praise
of *The Pilgrim* by asserting that it showed a return
to the artist's earlier and, by implication, cruder
manner.   That was not the present writer's feeling.   This film seemed to him a perfect example
of the principles of the screen-play, and as such
to be worthy of careful study.

Let us recall the theme in order to understand
the art of its presentment.   Briefly, *The Pilgrim*
was the story of an escaped convict who exchanges
his prison-dress for the clothes of the first bather
whom he meets upon his way.   These clothes
prove to be clerical.   So donned, Mr. Chaplin

(artfully varying the waiter's sable suit without which the children at least would hardly recognize him) makes for the nearest railway station. Every person that he meets seems to his disordered nerves a detective in mufti, the very grille of the ticket-office prison bars. Fortunately his disguise proves a passport to the inattention that his excitement threatens every instant to dispel, since strangers and officials regard the Cloth as a cloak for what, in a tweed suit, would be held an excessive timidity. He has taken a ticket and is settled in his seat when the back of his neighbour's paper tells him (and us) that a reward is already being offered for his arrest. His involuntary start and the spray of crumbs that issue from his lips at this discovery lead his neighbour to shift his position, in doing which a detective's star is revealed on the neighbour's coat, inside. The pilgrim retreats precipitately, to leave the train at the next station, which turns out to be that at which the real owner of the clothes was to arrive.

A contingent of parishioners awaits him with dutiful attentions. He is conducted to their place of worship, and invited, on the spot, to induct himself by taking an immediate service there. This peril he scrambles through, largely thanks to the indulgence with which the congregation regards a new pastor who is preternaturally shy. At extreme moments he produces his cigarette-case, and his embarrassment increases at every solecism. After the service is over and he is on the way to the Elder's house, he is recognized by a prison acquaintance who insists on being introduced also into the family.   The pilgrim is busy trying to protect their property from the unremitting attentions of his friend, but is finally arrested, conducted to a moorland waste, and there, to crown his adventures and to reward his recent virtue, he is given a kick : into freedom. On his bewildered and gradual awakening to the gift of his liberty the story ends.

The test of this summary will be how far, on re-reading it, the effect of a series of visible incidents shall have been given.   For the admirable simplicity of the story is not only in its artistic plausibility, but also in its optical allusiveness. It gave incomparable opportunities to Mr. Chaplin's powers of gesture, because it was conceived through his optic, not his other cranial, nerves.   Its Attic salt, of course, resided in his physiognomic rendering of it.   The gift of making much, and of avoiding the vulgar most, of very little, is the born comedian's top of accomplishment.   No one now needs to be reminded of Mr. Chaplin's technical resources.   This story also was a film-story. Virtually it did fulfil its author's boast of a film that told itself.   The number of verbal explanations thrown upon the screen was trifling. Some were almost superfluous.   The sermon was heralded by three words : David and Goliath (which proved hardly necessary).   The preacher mimed his sermon, by identifying himself in turn, briefly but sufficiently, with each antagonist. The primary appeal of all drama must be to the eye. A dramatic moment on the stage, even in Shakespeare who can be read for pleasure, is typically one that is seen almost before it is heard or felt.

The film, deliberately, limits itself to the sense of eyesight. The best film, therefore, is that which is the purest pantomime. In panto- mime, as we all know, Mr. Chaplin excels ; but he could not make the utmost of his executant's resources until films should have been imagined for pantomime, and not for acting. Therefore he began to compose them for himself. This order of development has given to him his supremacy. His method was not imposed from without but has grown naturally. By pantomime of course is meant, not that rude travesty, once miscalled the harlequinade, which perished of a surfeit of its own sausages, but dumb-show, the immemorial art of mumming (that is, dumb-showing).

Mr. Chaplin mums (to use the old word) with the whole of his body, and his body is controlled. like a good dancer's, by the imagination and the keen brain behind it. These two appear in the restraint with which the theme was handled. The hero of *The Pilgrim* might have been, very easily, the vulgar butt of a stupid caricature. Could even W. S. Gilbert or the author of *The Private Secretary* have been, off-handedly, entrusted with it ? The congregation and their Beulah might have been made equally tiresome, but in this film they could have recognized themselves without offence save in the fact of recognition.   This restraint in a farcical situation maintained the comedy.   It showed us what the art of the film can be, and was a model film-story.   It opened fascinating vistas, and history will do justice to the artist who made them possible.

If a film should contain no sensation or emotion that cannot be visibly presented and conveyed by pantomime, its limitation in this direction is compensated by its power to display actions that are incapable of becoming visible anywhere else. The whole world of the fantastic and the strange belongs to the film.   The whole of literature is denied to it.   Could we not persuade Mr. Chaplin to attempt the world of dreams, to give us some of the limitless resources of nightmare?   An author cannot think for long without reverting to books, but one may be pardoned for proposing a re-creation on the film of *The Confessions of an English Opium Eater*.   The book contains th idea, and the pleasures and pains of opium would translate themselves readily into images.   Something of the kind was attempted with great success, I am told, in *The Cabinet of Dr. Calli-Garri*, a film that I unfortunately missed.   Its subject was, I think, the distorted visions of a maniac, where the extravagances proper to the film must have been amazing.

All ideas should be banished from the film,

which cannot convey them.   Sensations are its
proper province.   I have never seen a film-version
of a novel that was not an outrage, that did not
omit its only points of interest.   Elaborate spectacles are equally tiresome, as tiresome as the
written version of the ordinary film-story would
be.   The art must respect its limitations if it is
to produce its hidden wealth ; and it would be
hard to conceive an author not disabled by his
profession for film production.   Most film-acting
is absurd and tedious because the actors are
attempting to convey emotions that are beyond
the scope of physiognomy.   Their bodies, not
their faces, are their instruments of expression,
and it is noteworthy that Mr. Chaplin never relies
on his countenance alone, but chooses by preference the emotion of embarrassment because this
is naturally expressed by the whole body, and can
be conveyed as readily by his back.   Subjects
that are suitable for the ballet are usually suitable
for the film, and we should be grateful to Mr.
Chaplin for having been one of the first producers
to turn his back on books and authors.   The
technique of the film is nearer to that of the dance,
and the world of fairyland, dreams, nightmares,
ritual, whatever can be imagined or presented in
dumbshow, is ample opportunity.

Mr. Chaplin's favourite gesture is one of embarrassment, his characteristic hero the poor
simpleton in a friendless world.   In his hands the
youngest of the arts has thus revived one of the

oldest of traditional figures. The Chaplin hero
is none other than the Holy Fool of other times.
Each of these pilgrims is your guileless Christian
on his progress through a wicked world, and if we
are asked where Christian art is to be seen alive
and stirring at the present day, the true answer
is upon the films of Mr. Chaplin. Perhaps that
is why his appeal is universal, and was first
recognized by the poor and the unlettered.

The best proof of the artistic virtue of the film
is that it appeals naturally to the illiterate. It
should be the fine art of illiteracy, and if none of
its spectators could read, it would have been
compelled to avoid most of its errors. Literature
is its natural enemy, and we must purge it of the
taint of the one art with which it can have nothing
in common.

THE WRITINGS OF FRANK HARRIS

THE vigour and robustness to be found in the writings of Mr. Frank Harris occur only in those uncommon authors who are primarily men of action. This characteristic quality of style is now explained on that page of his unfinished book, *My Life and Loves*, where he tells us that, at the age of fifteen, he used a sum of ten pounds won in a scholarship examination to pay his passage to America, a country at which he arrived unfriended and alone. Long before he turned author he had led an active and adventurous life, and before the age of twenty had amassed more experiences in different parts of the world than fill the lives of many quiet and stay-at-home people. The effect of these adventures on his imagination is apparent in his subsequently written books. His style is as effective as a display of singlestick, but his experience of the world deepened also a temperamental tenderness, so that in his writings he responds principally to two appeals, the appeals of distinction and of pity. The two themes cross and recross each other in his work. Indeed they mingle, for distinction easily becomes tragic since it is exceptional, and misfortune may ennoble its victims.   In both pity is not far at the moment when the distinction is felt.

When the temperament of the man of action is accompanied by a genuine literary gift, it always produces dramatic writing.   Mr. Harris would have written more plays if his own personality did not step between his pen and his characters when he tries to create them through the medium of speech.   Dialogue is not his strong point.   He can display a character in set speeches or separate remarks better than he can allow it to issue continuously in its own words.   His stories are all dramatic : his plays are like stories that have been dramatized.   In the novels and tales he is content with the action itself for his effect.   Consequently, even when he is moved to express his admiration or his pity, his pen moves a little roughly like a sword or a stick used to trace letters on the ground.   If his style were as fine as his sympathies, he would be a great writer, but his work suffers because his material of beauty, coming fresh from the quarry of life, remains a little rough.   In his own writings the raw material beguiles him more than the workmanship upon it.

Perhaps, like Rodin or Philip Webb, he is careful never to efface the facettings of the tool marks.   By this means he is able to render the illusion of fact and experience with a verisimilitude not easily to be surpassed, but sometimes at

the price of suggesting the quality of journalism at
its finest.   There remains with the reader a (perhaps deceptive) sensation of haste, as if the author
found his subject too pressing to admit of delay,
and must treat it vigorously in time for the next
edition.   He admires genius beyond all else in
the world, so much indeed that, though the
ambitions and combativeness of the active man
colour all his writings, no trace of envy is to be
found in them.   On the other hand, he seems
unexpectedly sensitive to his own originality, and,
for a spirit evidently generous in matters of
literature, inclined to fancy that others may be
plagiarizing his work, especially that part of
which he is most proud, his studies of Shakespeare.

The enduring reflections enforced by his books
are that nature and men combine to persecute all
distinction, and that nature punishes men and
women more severely for their slips than for their
offences.   From this he concludes that admiration and tolerance, the Hellenic worship of the
noble and the Christian lesson of lovingkindness,
are the two qualities of which the world stands
most in need.   These he would unite in a Pagan-
Christian system of ethics : a very interesting
idea.   The absence of these virtues in average
human beings and the blind indifference of Nature
produce, according to Mr. Harris, the tragedies
of life.

It is characteristic that the one story which Mr.

Harris has translated from Hans Andersen is the tale of the ugly duckling who proved to be a swan. If he had written the fable himself, the cygnet might have been fatally maimed by his purblind neighbours and family. In the *Yellow Ticket*, the volume in which this rendering occurs, we have stories of an innocent girl who could not be admitted to Christian Moscow unless she enrolled herself as a prostitute, because her purse was empty though her head was full ; of a youth whose diseased vision made the world so fantastically interesting that he became miserable when his eyesight was cured. In the end he was dissuaded from suicide by his observant, if cynical oculist, who told the boy that, if he cultivated the virtues, he and his fellows would seem as idiotic to each other as both had done before the oculist interfered.

Another favourite theme of the short stories is that of minorities, of exceptional or oppressed races and people. This has given to us several tales about the Jews. They are always treated sympathetically. In the tale of " Isaac and Rebecca " we are introduced to a young Jewess. She is eager for money ; her father apparently is not, but at the critical moment the old man yields to the intuition of his race, and so beguiles the wealthy banker into proposing. In *Unpath'd Waters*, the best volume of his short stories, there is the admirable tale of the old Jew who explained the art of making money. He realized, almost at his mother's knee, that it is the middleman who makes the money, and most quickly when he sells things that have no fixed price. So he began with old clothes. He went on to curiosities. He passed to works of art and became a dealer in antiques. He ended as a banker, for by selling money he found a commodity the price of which varies every day. It is a capital story. As an artistic lesson in economics it should be compared with Mr. Belloc's *Mercy of Allah*, in particular with the tale therein about the merchant of camels. In time of war the Sultan offers him paper money for his herd. The merchant returns to the Sultan a sack of slips on each of which is written " this is a camel." How long shall we have to wait before such stories are included in the study of economics at our schools ?

A Daughter of Eve is an admirable study of two sisters who are in love with the same man. It tells how the stronger, yielding to a momentary impulse of vanity, eventually sees in turn her sister and her brother-in-law attempt to drown themselves. It is, as the supposed narrator remarks, " just like life : no meaning in it ; the punishment out of all proportion to the sin." Before she died the impulsive girl proved a devoted woman, loved in her own home and admired for her public spirit by the world. There is no reason to suppose that Daisy's true character was revealed in the momentary impulse to which she yielded, or modified by the tragic results that followed this. She was too

strong to alter or to be crushed, but Nature chose
to punish heavily a caprice without which Daisy
would not have been entirely natural.

Montes the Matador is too well known to need
analysis to-day.   In *Elder Conklin*, the Sheriff and
his Partner is a flash-light picture gone before we
are aware of all that it means.   It is nearly a
perfect example of Wordsworth's dictum :

> Action is transitory—a step, a blow,
> The motion of a muscle this way or that—
> 'Tis done ; and, in the after vacancy,
> We wonder at ourselves like men betray'd.

The story shows what Mr. Harris can do with
incident, as Elder Conklin had shown how he
could depict a character.   Moreover, the other
side of the author's imagination exemplifies
Wordsworth's succeeding couplet :

> Suffering is permanent, obscure and dark,
> And shares the nature of infinity.

This brooding conviction has inspired many of
Mr. Harris's tales.

More qualified praise must be given to his
Shakespearean studies.   His prime qualification
is that he evidently knows most of the plays by
heart.   This intense familiarity led him to ask
what type of personality had created them.   His
powers of memory and divination enabled him to
evoke a portrait which is clear when he remembers
that it is the personality, rather than the life-story,

L

of the poet that the method reveals.   The method
breaks when employed to divine other real people,
such as Shakespeare's mother, who have left no
written record of themselves, and, unlike the Dark
Lady, were not the constant subject of Shakespeare's verse : on the various studies of the Dark
Lady Mr. Harris is plausible enough.   Indeed,
the method depends for its effectiveness precisely
upon its limitations.   It also assures us that
nothing in the legends that have come down about
the poet is out of character, for there is nothing
surprising in the feats of a precocious youth, if he
were Shakespeare.   To such a poet a vagabond
youth was a richer education than prolonged
schooling, and his natural appetite for reading
would be whetted by the extended instruction that
he lacked.   All his disadvantages, as they are
called, would be advantages to a man of genius.
It is therefore amusing to remember that only
men of no genius have professed to find them
insurmountable !   By the way, there may be
more than Mr. Shaw's little joke in the title *As You
Like It*, a play with a double motive originally
acted by an actor in disguise.

    Like much of Mr. Harris's characteristic work,
The Man Shakespeare, is a vivid piece of portraiture.   When he knows a character thoroughly,
by intuition or in life, he is an admirable draughts-
man.   His life of Wilde is likely to be final, and
is one of his vivid and courageous books.

    Where his admiration or sympathy is aroused,

Mr. Harris is a writer with a tender conscience. This is touched to the quick by nobility of thought or the persecution of weakness. The latter horrified him when the Chicago anarchists were the victims, and he so told their story in *The Bomb* as to immortalize its memory. If vividness were the whole of narrative, and candour all that men require in the presentation of passion, this novel would rank very high for it has both. The story could not be more vigorously told, but if the reader does not yield himself entirely to its movement and manfully preserves his critical sense, he lays the book down at last with the feeling that it is a masterpiece rather of reporting than of literature. If journalism were half as good as this, we should have excellent excuses for the time that we waste upon it. There is a distinction. Even the best journalism fails to touch the deepest springs. It suffers from an excess of excitement. It lacks the last achievement of repose, which is the moment when writing passes into literature. In *The Bomb* the events, the characters, their motives and feelings are set down in broad strokes with the effect of a superb poster.

A better novel is *Great Days*, its author's most artistic achievement in the longer forms of prose narrative. Against the background of the Napoleonic wars, a distant shadow that lends repose and dignity to the busy foreground of the story, we have a lively picture of the smugglers and merchant seamen on both the Channel coasts.

These revolve round two centres of human interest, an English and a French family. They complement and contrast each other, and bring the characters of the two nations into relief. Every figure in each family we learn to know and understand, and event grows from event with unfaltering interest. It is odd that its author's most artistic creation seems not to have run into many editions. Perhaps his death, the last favour that fate confers upon an artist's reputation, will make known the merit of this book. The historical scene of *Great Days* is conveyed by a few deftly placed touches : the arrival of the napkin from France ; the controversy over the right number of pommels on a side-saddle ; the glimpses of Bonaparte and Fox.

On the subject of the Corsican, Fox says : " Successful men are never so great as they are made out to be. It's like judging a man by his shadow. . . . Great men are usually richer in temperament than Bonaparte appears to be, and richer in faults, too. . . . I did not wish to combat French ideas which seemed to me just and right. But now that Bonaparte is making himself a despot I should have no hesitation." On the idea of equality : " How would it be if there could be equality or a great approach to equality in necessaries, while keeping all the distinctions as honours. . . . Honours would be more esteemed if they could not be won by money." The opinions of the imaginary figures

are equally in character, though they all tend to
speak in the same vigorous way, and as a work of
art *Great Days* is Mr. Harris's best novel.

His heroes are generally men of action, or
imaginative people to whom action is made a
martyrdom because they stir the world by their
thoughts and words.   To him particularly, words
are the activity of thought ; beauty and truth
causes to be fought and died for.   This energy of
soul has occasioned one witty definition : " A
gentleman, to me, is a thing of some parts but no
magnitude :   one should be a gentleman and
much more."   Louis Lingg in *The Bomb* makes a
somewhat parallel statement, no less indicative of
his creator's mind : " The writer tries to find a
characteristic word ; the painter some scene that
will enable him to express himself.   I always
wanted a characteristic deed."   Mr. Harris's
volumes are much like deeds.   Each is meant to
incite to action by the spell of its image or its idea,
to imprint impressions that will last, like a thing
seen, a thrilling experience, a personal revelation.
Each book is intended to have on the reader " the
tonic touch " of the experience itself.

The man of action is reputed to be dumb at
moments of emotional crisis.   Indeed, the
author's most convincing example, Elder Conklin,
is articulate only in his prayers.   His silence is
broken, so to speak, by his swift, unhesitating
decisions.   If this be true of such men, has Mr.
Harris too much in common with the active tem-

perament to find unforgettable phrases of beauty for the furthest reaches of his thought ?   It must be something of this kind that makes our reluctant qualifications necessary.   The substance is often so good that we seem cheated of some quality in the treatment.   Yet there is a tonic virtue in its denial.   We do occasionally find actions that are like poems : the number of books with the quality of living tissue is hardly more numerous.   Men of action can often write well.   The rare thing is that such a temperament should devote itself to the practice of literature.   When this happens (Florence Nightingale is a classic example) the writings have the gust of a sea-breeze.

In Mr. Harris's stories, the lovers are creatures of desire trying to rise into creatures of feeling. He gives to us the alphabet of passion, but the separate letters are always struggling to compose themselves into intelligible love.   In *Elder Conklin*, Loo is a sketch compared with Ida in *The Bomb*, or Margaret Barron in *Great Days*.   Mr. Harris has readier intuitions of his men, but the tender core beneath the rind of his temperament enables him to divine his heroines, of whom he writes with the fondness of a father for a favourite child.   His heroines are those most likely to appeal to a thoughtful man of action, and they are depicted either passionately or with the tenderness that the proverbial soldier extends to children.

The volumes of *Contemporary Portraits* are very unequal, and more suggestive of hasty improvisation, possibly for the benefit of the American public, than any other of his works.   Since his anecdotes are generally in character, their alleged invention does not much matter.   They are, generally, dramatically right, and some licence is usually conceded to writers of reminiscences about famous, and therefore much debated, people. What may be written in haste is necessarily read with reservation.

Bernard Shaw has often suggested that Frank Harris should write his autobiography, but the first volume raised questions that cannot be discussed in a final paragraph.   It is more like a bomb than any of his books, as if Casanova had timed his work to explode in the twentieth century. Only those capable of controlling their prejudices will be able to read it at all.   Those incapable will not read far.   Autobiographies fall into two classes : those of the adventurous and those of the introspective man.   There is a middle category, filled by the reflective man of letters, a rank to which the introspective writer (being partly sterile) rarely wins.   Cellini and Casanova are examples of the first ; Rousseau and Gibbon of the middle order ; Amiel, Barbellion, Marie Lénéru of the introspective type.   Mr. Harris's life and confessions belong to the adventurous class.   In deed and word he is wholly unashamed, but, as he is a man of intelligence, he gives us a series of reflections in support of this procedure.   These are deeply felt, and not to be dismissed lightly.

The valid contention in his preface is that languages can die of euphemisms, and that nineteenth-century English suffered from them. The objection to his latest practice is that the vocabulary of corner-boys is no remedy. Some selection is the beginning of all literature ; and, while a sincere man of letters must hold that there is no fact or fancy that literature cannot describe, yet he will add that the more physical you choose to be the less fit is the vocabulary of hooligans. With the world's literature before us, there is abundant proof that the coarsest of great writers never did write like corner-boys. The penalty of those who do is to be found unendurable by every one else. What a pity that a violent, if intelligible, reaction should destroy a perfectly valid plea for candour. Between euphemisms and the terms of the gutter the way of literature is perfectly clear. The masculine tongue of classic writers is as free from one as from the other.

At best, he has attempted in his old age that which he would have had done for himself by others in his youth, and that must be his condonation. When the man of action possesses also the power of communicating his experiences and their lessons, his writings have a way of surviving the criticisms that they arouse. In sum, Mr. Harris's works, from first to last, illustrate the maxim of Santayana, that " to turn events into ideas is the function of literature."

Looking back over his work, I recommend him

as a stimulating author, a man with a wider than the average English view, a courageous man, a blunt man, whose vivid, rough, essentially dramatic, imagination gives to words the living quality of action.   He has the faculty of the keen eye-witness, who is neglected to-day because he has excited strong distaste, wilfully, indeed, in part, but still more by his determination to make us see the other side of questions which we prefer to view through the darkened glasses of political or moral prejudices.   Other authors go for the hearts, more rarely the heads, of their readers. Mr. Harris, like a boxer, goes straight for the epigastrium, and the luckless reader, when he has found his breath once more, has no choice but to run away or begin another bout.   Neither alternative is without its humiliations, and, for the future, the reader usually resolves to leave this formidable person alone.   Mr. Harris's pen is too devastating for the average English taste, which in political, biographical, and critical writings, much prefers authors who omit as many debatable issues as possible.   The Englishman's castle is a dark old house, and he becomes indignant when anyone lets a ray of light enter one of its cherished gloomy corners.   Yet the criticism, say of our educational ideals in the pamphlet entitled *How to Beat the Boers*, is still alive and worth having.

VERS LIBRE

IN his preface to *Otherworld : Cadences*, Mr. F. S. Flint defended vers libre by saying : "There is only one art of writing, and that is the art of poetry ; and wherever you feel the warmth of human experience and imagination in any writing, there is poetry, whether it is in the form we call prose, or in rhyme and metre, or in the unrhymed cadence," in which the book containing this preface is mostly written. Again, he says, "All our best prose writers are poets." Only uncritical people will be unsympathetic to Mr. Flint, or will deny (without supplying definitions) the term "poetry" to much of his writing, elsewhere and here. Yet surely Shelley was a poet in his verse in a sense that he was not a poet in his letters, and if poetry has been, as Mr. Flint insists, too much confused with rhyme and metre, Mr. Flint's reaction therefrom involves us in another kind of confusion ? Is it possible, with the aid of a few definitions, to put our ideas in clearer order ?

All speech falls into rhythm of which there are three principal types : measured rhythm or metre, the traditional form of verse, the non-metrical or

discontinuous rhythms of prose, and antithetical
prose (or cadence) which is a cross between them.
By antithetical prose I mean the complementary
cadence in which, for example, much of the
Authorized Version is written.   Examples of
measured rhythm or metre are needless.   The
works of Swift and Addison are convenient
examples of strict prose, prose, that is, which is to
the least possible extent metrical, and the substance of which is not generally poetic.   Modern
examples of antithetical prose (or cadence) abound
in the works of Ruskin or Walt Whitman.   The
latter did not invent a new form.   He reverted to
an old original.   The rhythm of such cadence is
as unmistakable as that of metre.   Ruskin's

To fix for a little the foam upon the river * and to make the
ripples everlasting upon the lake,

is as obviously in complementary cadence as

The Lord is king,* be the people never so impatient
He sitteth between the cherubim,* be the earth never so unquiet.

Whitman's lines upon animals, such as

They do not make me sick * discussing their duty to God

will serve as a reminder of the complementary
cadence, which was the form that he made his own.
If all speech falls into one or other of the three
types of rhythm mentioned, then we should be
able to say to which any particular example
belongs.   But, after we shall have recognized its
rhythmical form, we shall not yet be in a position

to say whether or not it is poetry.   Two further
considerations remain to be decided.   Mr. Flint
readily admits that metre is not enough, and has
no difficulty in showing that the line

I thee do love, my darling. Be thou mine !

is not poetry.   But, on the other hand, his remark,
" all our best prose writers are poets," would
include Swift's *Tracts* and *The Spectator* among
poetry, and that would be equally extravagant.
In other words, Mr. Flint, having shown that
metre and rhyme are not enough to make poetry,
implies that substance, without these, is enough.
If it were, metre would hardly have been invented.

Besides this, there are prosaic thoughts, no less
than prosaic words, and such thoughts, however
well expressed, as we see (for example) in sections
of Wordsworth, do not suffice to make poetry
with or without the aid of measured rhythm.
For poetry, then, at least some measured rhythm
or cadence is necessary, and poetic substance too.
Even these do not suffice, however, for you may
have a poetic thought expressed in either, yet, if
the language or diction be weak, the result is not
poetry.   It is only when all three factors are
present (and they are rarely found perfectly in all
three degrees) that we find unchallengeable
poetry.   The advantage of insisting upon all
three, when critically examining the subject, is
that it furnishes us with a means, of reasonable
precision, to distinguish the several forms of

poetry, prose and cadence, and more or less exactly to define where one lapses into another in examples upon the debatable borderland. Mr. Flint identifies Cadence with Vers Libre. Since the latter, eager to escape from metre (we need not insist here on the absence of rhyme) mixes the ingredients, we shall find it approaching to one or the other, and often to prose ; it never for long, except perhaps in Mr. Flint's work which is carefully revived cadence, is true to any. A glance backward shows us how this desire to veer has come about.

The modern tendency to vers libre among English writers can be dated conveniently from Henley's *A Late Lark Twitters in the Quiet Skies*. Though this began by the rejection of rhyme, it keeps, as the opening line shows, close to metre. Since then, the tendency has been to depart more and more from metre into one, or both, of the other types of rhythm mentioned above. Vers libre, then, has not invented a new form nor merely revived an old one. It has rejected one of the three constituents of poetry, namely metre, in favour of a mixture of the other two. The cadence, that Mr. Flint favours, somewhat resembles, because he is not as strict as were his professed originals, the cursus, or regular metrical ending to sentences, which has been traced in Latin prose, but has never been formally used in English except, Professor A. C. Clark reminds us, in the English collects. If this statement be just,

the writer of vers libre will tend to veer more and
more from measured rhythm to the discontinuous
rhythms of prose, since even the cadence, which is
a paired series of complementary rhythms with
usually identical accents, will seem too metrical for
him.   More than this, he will tend to turn away
not only from the rhythms familiar in poetry, but
from traditional subjects of poetry also ; and, in
consequence, his temptations will be to become
prosaic no less in substance than in rhythm ; for
the subject-matter of poetry is not unlimited.
This, I think, has often happened ; and such
recoil as there has been from vers libre, where it
was not simply prejudice, has been a perhaps
imperfectly conscious impatience as much with
the matter as with the manner of the new school.
Indentation, which is only punctuation in another
form, can mark a cadence, but can hardly create
one.   Where no true cadence exists, indentation
is as truly an external contrivance as the formal
metre that it replaces.

If the day comes, and I hope it will, when prose
is studied as explicitly as verse, readers will hesitate
to admit to the category of prose (having a nicer
term to express their peculiar pleasure in them)
many of the passages to which imperfectly critical
enthusiasts now point when they wish to assert
that verse and prose are one art.   Just as all
speech falls into rhythm, so all thought or matter
of speech has its rhythm also.   In the main, the
prose poem has coupled a poetical thought or, its

poor relation, a witty idea to an antithetical or semi-metrical rhythm. If you throw away one of the three constituents of poetry, you must clearly strengthen the two others. And if you throw away two of these elements, namely metre and substance, the finest diction will hardly make a poem. We do not quarrel with writers of vers libre for making " moods " their subject ; but, should metre and diction be alike absent or undistinguished, we become acutely critical of the quality of the mood expressed. Such writers are fond of taking subjects like the vague mood of a man in a bath, the vague mood induced by looking through a rain-splashed window, or by watching a queue outside a moving-picture house. Where the mood is more defined, as, for instance, the mood of excitement induced by the lights and sounds of the traffic in a great city, the element of repose, always necessary in art to the tensest mood of excitation, is often lacking ; and, criticizing it, we remember that, had it been expressed in metre, the repose would have been given by the metre itself.

Because the laws of English prosody are still obscure (so that metrists, for example, disagree on the correct scansion of the first line in *Paradise Lost*, though the ear recognizes it to be, apart from the great authority of its author, a true example of blank verse) people try to write by ear alone. The ear seems the only certain test of a doubtful English line in any English metre, upon the problems of which Mr. T. S. Omond has shed more light than any recent student known to me. In an as yet unpublished paper, a scholar of my acquaintance has discussed *The Ingredients of Latin and English Verse*. This he kindly allowed me to read when I had begun to make notes for this discussion. My friend bases his argument on the three constituents mentioned ; his second, diction, was an addition to my notes. The moral, therefore, seems to be that writers of vers libre should be more careful than they often are of the quality of their subjects and of their diction the more they seek to depart from metre or even cadence, which, being a short rhythm repeated twice in succession, is a fragment or series of fragments of metre. They might also become less impatient of the charge of writing in prose, since the rejection of metre allows them no alternative but prose or cadence. We shall only be uttering shrill words to one another until we define the only forms of rhythm available, and realize that none of the three elements of poetry suffices by itself, and that, where one has been rejected, the other two must be strengthened ; and if metre and diction are both rejected, as some vers librists reject them, then the subject is of overweening importance, though, to those who would think clearly, the subject alone, even of a national anthem, can never suffice to make a poem.

It is in doubtful and experimental cases that definitions help.

LITTERÆ HUMANIORES

UNLESS the double scope of this term is
borne in mind, criticism grows anæmic by
losing touch with the humane element in letters.
The term is one that marries two divergent tendencies, the tendency toward thought and theory
(litteræ) and the tendency toward observation
and manners (humaniores). Humane literature
dwells on the life of the market-place and on the
learning of the study with equal lovingness, so
that, in so far as literature has the power to
humanize a man at all, it will develop the sympathies of all sides of his nature. Since art is
man's best teacher, for man is influenced through
his imagination and all powerful influence is
indirect, letters, the most comprehensive of the
arts, must be the art best adapted to a liberal
education. This would be more obvious than it
is did not many who carry off the prizes of the
schools none the less remain insensible to the
classical spirit. But that is to say only that if the
finest types are necessarily rare, those who can
benefit from the fullest human training are hardly
less rare.

When we look back, who is sure that he himself did wisely to risk an elementary education ? When it is a matter of the humanities, the character is as necessary to the training as the training is to the character. In practice, therefore, all we could do would be to expect nothing, but to give the most pertinacious applicant his chance. The value of the intellectual element in literature needs no emphasis. Indeed it has become emphasized too much, that is to say at the expense of its co-equal, the humane. At present, it is the humane element that needs apology ; for it is the mark of the mere prizeman to be insensible to its value, thereby to invite the gibe which Johannes Secundus threw in the faces of the Grammarians ; that, namely, he wrote with licence in order that his work might not become a chopping-block for commentators nor a lesson-book for schoolboys. One of the best novels in the world is the *Satyricon* of Petronius. Cannot this be rescued from the two classes of men who mainly study it ; those who have too much scholarship and no humanity, and those who have no scholarship at all ?

In what does the pleasure of reading it consist ? First, in the astonishing invention which passes before us a series of incidents conceived so happily as to be humorous without being improbable, and, second, because these are discussed and described in an idiom that fits each character like a glove. As some one has said well, the book gives to Roman literature that which the vase-painters gave to Greek pots, an art of *genre*, as homely as a child's play, as racy as a gipsy's patter : the rarest, as it is the priceless, gift of authorship. Much of the humour is as coarse as are the characters which display it ; many feel it too coarse to-day, because, though coarseness is the simplest element of humour, it is a mistake for any one element to be overdone. Only those who have never read such works forget that the scope of grossness is limited.

But that we speak of Petronius when we speak of Aristophanes, Rabelais and Boccaccio proves the perduring quality of his book. Some say that all these authors, though men of genius, would have been greater had they eschewed that ingredient which their names suggest to vulgar people (and to no one else). The fellow who wishes to dictate the practice of the man he calls a Master has a right to his opinion ; so have the rest of us to our opinion of *him*. The real answer to this criticism, I think, is that there has been (observe, I do not say that there now is, or make any prophecy for the future) a unanimity of practice among the greatest masters which must command our respect.

It suggests, though it does not prove, that coarseness is the root of all humour ; in any case great literature is known by a catholic sympathy for *both* extremes of man's desires. How far this reflection will carry him the reader himself may take the remainder of his days to reflect. They could, perhaps, be spent less profitably. The value of the *Satyricon* lies, the value of the humane element in literature lies, in bringing back letters, reflection, to its simple roots in human nature, and these roots, like any others, are none the less important because they are unfitted for the raw reader and for prolonged exposure to the light.

Human nature is the embrace of the body and the spirit. Theologically speaking, the Incarnation is the affirmation in which the two are reconciled. Until the word shall have been made flesh, and the flesh word, each is unassimilable. The flesh is the simpler of the two, as the root is simpler than the flower, even though " the root exists for the flower and not the flower for the root."[1] The simplicity of the body is the source of humour. Humour differs from wit in the supersession of intellect by a sympathetic quality, in virtue of which it becomes akin to reverence and even pathos. Humour, then, because it is simple is naturally broad, and because it is broad it contributes more than any other element to the humane division of letters.

We can conceive a man to argue that the *Satyricon* would be preferable if it omitted some of its incidents, and in support of his view he might point to *Gil Blas*, Cellini, George Borrow, or Mr. W. H. Davies, in all of whom the liveliness is retained though the coarseness is largely, or in the modern authors wholly, lacking. No one

[1] Coventry Patmore.

who is sensitive to the appeal of such literature, to the sense of adventurous life which pervades it, to the delightful simplicity of the characters, to the freedom-giving breath which makes their doings exhilarating, to the racy idiom of their talk, need deny this. But he will insist upon a qualification. He will reply that their adventures are not those which are expected to happen to " respectable " people, that the characters are mostly rascals, that their clowning is something barbarous, that the freedom is beyond the law, and that the talk is fundamentally, and in its narrow sense, immoral.

He will add further that the charm of the whole lies precisely in its freedom from all those bonds which wise men most cherish, except in occasional moments, throughout life. But these occasional moments, he will say, are as real as any other : the simpler appetites are no less genuine than that other appetite which desires to control them, in sum, therefore, that they and it, being equally real, are equally proper to literature. It has been wittily said that " the function of vice is to keep virtue within reasonable bounds."[1] The application of this dictum to letters means that when literature reaches one of its recurrent phases of over-sophistication ; when it busies itself too much with the flowers and fruits and too little with the roots and soils, then the appetites with their kindred humours, supply a wholesome corrective.

[1] Samuel Butler's *Notebooks*.

For literature, like life, can die of anæmia no less than of apoplexy. In a liberal education the humours are specially important, because the appetites, which will not be denied, demand in youth some outlet, and a convenient outlet for them is through letters, where they can be satisfied vicariously. At that period, and for the protected type of youth to which a liberal education is confined, with his carefully pruned prejudices, the humours of classic literature educate his sympathies by bringing him, vicariously, into the open stream of life, to remind him that the university of most of his fellows is the market-place, of which he knows nothing at first hand, with which he ought to be acquainted, and of which he is likely to learn intimately only through this channel of literature.

In the market-place, thus described for him by some of the liveliest pens in history, human instincts are seen without disguise, without sophistication ; and those appetites, which are the source of his own energy, are exposed in all their candour. In contact through literature with this simplicity, a man will become cleansed from much insincerity, as humour alone can cleanse him, and see himself for what he is : indifferent honest, one whose rules of honour are aspirations often beyond his reach. An appetite can be educated only by being drawn into the open, and provided with a proper outlet. The simpler appetites are no exception to this rule. To see them, as they are displayed in the literature that we have in mind, in a usurped control of the whole man, will warn him, if he be capable of the warning (and, if not, experience itself will prove in vain), that, if he indulges them unduly, he will become like those of whom it is instructive and amusing to read, but whose way of life it would be ruinous to follow. To have arrived at this alphabet of wisdom is a great gain, and for sophisticated people literature is the best way by which, in health and sincerity, it can be reached.

Thus, when comparing later authors with Petronius, say, we see that their books have the same root, and perform the same office as his own, except that they subdue an element that in him became dominant. That subdual does not alter their character. They imply much which they do not state. Not the substance, only the phrasing, has been emasculated. Occasionally they achieve miracles. Once, for instance, and outside humour altogether, in the writing of Mr. Davies, there are lines so simple as would be jarring in any writer less ingenuous than he, lines which seem to have strayed from the humanistic age as if to remind us afresh that, in matters of taste, simplicity of touch is alone infallible.

Since however, the humane element of letters is the simpler, as the reflective element is the more subtle, the root of the humane, though it needs recognition, may seem less than its fellow to need restatement in every century. Because it is crude

it is constant, and because it is constant it is free
from change.   Only the starveling, thought, can
grow ; humour and beauty are eternal.   Therefore many are satisfied with the ancient classics
for its expression, and seek restatement only for
that which may be termed its romantic or adventurous side.   This last is concerned not with
crude appetite, but with crude manners ; and,
manners, however crude, change with place, race,
and century.

Thus Petronius, whose merit lies in this double
presentation, is succeeded, in the delineation of
the manners of the market-place, by the picaresque
novels and memoirs of succeeding centuries ;
from Petronius down the ages to Mr. Pickwick.
The place of these in humane letters is unchal-
lenged.   The place of litteræ (thought and theory)
is their peculiar pride.   It has remained to
remind ourselves that the *humaner* letters, the
object of which is to complete the whole man and
to cultivate every element in his nature, have been
called *humaniores* because they also include the
cultivation not of manners only, but of appetite.

Their proud claim is their claim to catholicity ;
and we who have learned to respect its justice and
to realize its use, have this for our reward : that
we are safe to soar with Plato because we have
walked the streets with Petronius, and may
safely plan a pinnacle of thought toward heaven
because its base has been set securely in the earth,
so that the flower of our humanity blossoms fairly

because its radicles have been nourished on the simplest food, braced by the wind of humour, and enriched by the animal matter which here finds its worthy function, and has therefore gained for its literary husbandman the reward of immortality. Because his function is simple, his service is great. To recognize its nature is to apprehend that which he has to teach us, and the reason why he has been given his own niche in the temple of fame, where he has been subject to fewer fluctuations of regard than any wholly respectable author.

THE AUTHOR'S TOOL

L ITERATURE is the one art which possesses no handicraft. What is the effect of this on literary style ? The receipt of a bill from a Midland bookseller from whom I had made some purchases decisively drew my attention to this subject. The details in his bill of the books which had been ordered were written in a beautiful penmanship, and when the receipt arrived it was a pleasure to notice that the terms of acknowledgment were written in the same lettering as the printed name and address of the bookseller at the top of the sheet. Apparently the fount of type had been designed from his handwriting. This delighted me so much that I wrote a letter saying that I had not hitherto supposed it possible for anyone to add to the pleasure of an ordinary receipt. Thereupon the following letter arrived. It deserves to be quoted as an example of a simple, commercial transaction beautifully done. Readers, however, must be content with the substance which, stripped of its beautiful form, read as follows :

" Accept my thanks for your kind letter and

remittance.   Your words of praise gave me great pleasure, and I thank you for them.   Caligraphy has been my delight since childhood, and is still my greatest joy and consolation.   I get plenty of scribbling now, since I am almost alone in this little book-business, yet compared to the output of authorship my efforts are tiny in comparison."

Alas ! compared to the delicate page on which his words are written, what countless printed pages are put to shame.   My correspondent had found the practice of penmanship not only a " delight since childhood," but a " consolation " in later life.

The author's tool then was no exception : its handling also had agreeable secrets of its own. Though my own handwriting is past blaming, I dipped into the subject and found that to acquire a good formal hand was, strictly speaking, the occupation of a lifetime.   A hobby may become that to a sincere amateur of any subject, but a more cursory study will give to anyone a new delight in handwriting, a new pleasure in printed books, and make him pause—to the surprise of other people —over tombstones.   The lettering upon an eighteenth-century tombstone often raises it to the dignity of literature.   These pleasures have brought in their train a friendship with a scribe, and made apparent certain elementary truths concerning the relation of penmanship to printing which, however obvious to professional students, are unheeded by the generality of writers.

The gulf between writing and printing is so wide
that it requires a mental effort at first to form a
bridge between them.   Reading is a confirmed
habit in an age of newspapers ; groups of words
are read rapidly in a single glance.   Therefore it
is hardly surprising that those who have lost the
need to observe the shape of a letter should have
become blind to that subtler thing, its form.   Yet
the early printed books drew their beauty from the
manuscripts on which their founts of types were
modelled ; and after printing was established
penmanship,   handwriting,   began   to   decay.
Writers on the subject remark that there soon
became no living model for the type-founders ;
and that the founts became debased till they
reached their lowest point in the books printed in
the first half of the past century.   Handwriting
had ceased to be the scholar's art, and at present a
beautifully written letter, a letter even showing
care for clarity, spacing, and margin, gives us
mainly the pleasure of surprise.   The consequences are many.   Authors write now not to be
read, but to be printed ; and no one who has been
inside a printing office can doubt that if most
manuscripts were printed as they are received
they would be almost unintelligible.   A certain
well-known coroner, for instance, is indefatigible
in sending detailed reports of his remarks to an
editor of my acquaintance, but as these are
scrawled on the back of the newspaper cutting
which refers to the case in question, a distressing

inquest has to be held upon each. The hybrid jargon of the newspapers, the prevalence of commercial metaphors, the grotesque attempts at punctuation, the fatal habit of using euphemisms, are some of the results which necessarily follow the neglect of handwriting.

Anyone who devotes a few hours even to the rudiments necessary for the acquisition of a formal hand will make discoveries which conflict with the canons of the schoolroom and copy-book. He will find at once that every effect does, indeed, depend upon the pen ; and if he should happen to have a scribe among his friends he will become familiar with the lamentation that the pen " gave out " before a certain page was finished, and that painful hours were spent before a new one was cut to the nicety required by the texture of the paper obtainable. He will also learn that his governess had been unprofessional in teaching him never to remove the pen from the paper during the formation of a single letter, and that, for instance, such a simple letter as " e " is made by the scribe in three strokes. It is interesting also to realize how the pen has controlled the form of letters, and to learn, pen in hand, that the apparent difference between the form of Roman capitals and that of small letters is not arbitrary, but that the smaller became what they are simply through the attempt of the writer to trace the capitals at a high speed. Authorities relate that some, if not all, of the famous manuscripts, like the Book of Kells, were

not written slowly for all their care, but at a speed
which was the reward of constant practice. It
appears, too, that those who have revived the art
of penmanship in England have learnt most of its
secrets, as was to have been expected, from the use
of the pen itself ; and that certain beautiful serifs
and hooks at the end of the stems or tails of letters
can be formed only by a turn of the pen, which is a
true sleight of hand, the perfection of long
practice.

Unless people have a liking for early printed
books or have handled manuscripts, a piece of
script when first shown to them conveys nothing
but a puzzling sense of oddity. It seems to
require an effort of the will to direct the eyes from
the page to its component words, and from the
words to the letters.   Once this attention to detail
has become the first object of interest, it is evident
that every word, and every line, have received
separate attention.   Two forms of the same letter
will be used according to the presence or absence
of letters with stems or tails in the same or an
adjoining word ; ampersands will be used at dis-
cretion ; the cross strokes of " ts " at the end of
lines will be long or short according to the length
of the line itself compared with the length of
others.   The whole page thereby gains an effect of
balance, indeed of animation, which is the reverse
of the ordinary uniformity of print.   Each page
of script (and the same is true, but in a smaller
degree, of fine printing) becomes alive and indivi-

dual, with an interest and a character of its own.
Soon the variety of the varied forms becomes
delightfully familiar, and a challenge is opposed
to the quality, the literary quality, of the text.
Insincerity, nonsense, vulgarity is really made
aware of itself when brought into the beautiful
prominence of fine lettering. Writing was once
a vocation : penmanship the scholar's art ; for
the virtues of the scribe and of the writer are the
same, correctness, distinctness and order. If,
therefore, authors wrote to be read and not merely
to be printed, would they not write better in a
double sense ? Haste, inconsideration is the
enemy, not only of penmanship, but of style.

Throughout, the influence of the tool, the pen
itself, is seen to be potent. At first manuscripts
would not have been laboriously copied (Thomas
à Kempis, who belonged to the Brothers of the
Common Life, had " an exquisite hand," and is
said to have copied the whole Bible in four fat
volumes with his own pen), unless they contained
something which satisfied the imagination of men.
It was once customary that only scribes or Rabbis
of great sanctity should be allowed to copy the
sacred Christian or Jewish books. The form and
content of literature were one. The effect of
printing cannot be said to have improved the
quality of either. It has made the best more
accessible, and multiplied indefinitely the worst.

As the gulf widens between the art of literature
and the craftsmanship of the pen, both lose and

are oddly influenced by their loss. Of the decay
of beautiful handwriting it is not necessary to
speak ; and a modern, well-designed fount of
type comes to most of us with an air of self-con-
sciousness which proves that our eyes have become
impatient of observing the form of print. One
wishes, however, that more modern founts were
modelled upon eighteenth-century lettering, which
is as clear as it is beautiful, and does not dis-
turb the eye with the appearance of archaism.
John Baskerville's more modern founts need no
mention here ; and we need to go no further
than the nearest old churchyard for suggestions
of beautiful italic.

In respect of prose, when we look back to the
crows of triumph which heralded the New Journalism of the 'eighties, our judgment begins to
measure the degree of advantage in that change.
The decay of handwriting gave encouragement to
the typewriter ; the form of its letters was first
conditioned by the need to make them all of the
same width, and the typewriter has led the way to
shorthand and encouraged the habit of dictation,
which enables a man to write a book without ever
putting pen to paper. The divorce is thus complete : haste becomes a habit.

It is hardly too much to say that the click of the
typewriter makes itself heard in the mechanical
noise of a style such as that of Mr. Shaw, and a
new light was thrown upon the later style of Henry
James when it was recorded that the last involu-

tions of his manner were encouraged when the practice of dictation grew upon him. Walter Pater's parenthetical style developed with his habit of writing on alternate lines of ruled paper. Patmore's condensation was probably encouraged by his habit of writing on half sheets of note-paper, which sheets themselves were largely the outcome of scattered thoughts recorded upon envelopes and cuffs. George Moore dictates to a stenographer, but he has admitted that " the quality " of his prose is conferred by his holograph corrections : the dictated passages form the skeleton only. Pope's minute calligraphy, crowded upon odds and ends of paper, seems appropriate to one who was to perfect the couplet, and to make conciseness the chief quality of his style.

In fine, although literature, to its great loss, is the one art which possesses no handicraft, its result, like that of its more fortunate rivals, is still governed by the author's tool. Since, whether it be the pen, the typewriter, or the stenographer's pencil, that tool will influence the result, the case seems clear that, at some time in their careers, men of letters should be writers. A larger subject follows : the effect of printing on literature, and the degree to which literature is now controlled by the number of readers which the printing-press has placed within its reach.

N

THE EFFECT OF PRINTING ON LITERATURE

WE think that we know too well the extent of our debt to Caxton to reflect, as a rule, upon the remoter consequences of the invention of printing. The advantages of a multiplication of manuscripts are obvious. The disadvantages are also worth a moment's thought. To begin with, the multiplication of anything leads us into the realm of arithmetic, a mystic science, not only because certain numbers have a peculiar significance whereby we call three and seven " mystic numbers," but because the mere multiplication of anything changes its character. For example, a fine house is a fine thing, but a row of similarly designed fine houses is detestable. In repetition itself there seems to be something ominous. This is a fact which every one knows, and no one can explain. All we can say is that quantity and quality seem to be by nature hostile to each other. Perhaps the advantages and disadvantages of the invention of printing can be summarized fairly in the statement, that printing has made the best books more accessible and multiplied indefinitely

194

the worst. But before we consider whether a general accessibility of the best books is free from disadvantage, and whether the multiplication of bad books is something gained, we must remember that the influence of numbers has been apparent, not only in the increase of books printed, but also in the increase of readers. Multiplication of population soon followed multiplication of books. Consequently, when estimating the effect of printing on literature, we must consider the result upon the printed word of a growing multitude of readers. Each of the two numerical factors plays into the other's hands, and, when we ask whether to-day the multitude controls the printed word or the printed word the multitude, at first it may not seem easy to decide. The answer, I think, is, that whatever agent controls the printing-press, the number of readers controls the quality of the printed thing by the law of diminishing returns.

All conversions cut both ways ; the conversion of a savage to the ways of Western industrial life is, to some extent, a conversion of these ways of life to the savage, if not to savagery. Colonists tell us that the Westernized native is neither a true native nor a true Westerner, but a kind of hybrid, which sometimes reverts to a lower type than that of either of its unmixed elements. To any body of persons, or school of thought, recruits may be a source of weakness, a fact of experience which should caution all men of conviction against the popular belief that there is necessarily advantage in numbers.

When printing was first invented, only a small proportion of persons could read or write. These acquirements were still the scholar's arts, and, in consequence, were mainly won by those who most desired them. Since will, not mere desire, creates capacity, those (in and about the age of Caxton) who could read were likely to be those with a capacity to gain from reading, a rarer capacity than is supposed. Therefore the books printed, like the books written (new printed books were few at first), were designed for lovers of letters, and the only books to print were works that had already survived the test of time. Authors and readers were as nearly a homogeneous and equal body as they have ever been. One standard was common to both, and that a high one. The accessibility of the best books made these familiar. Familiarity created a desire for new books, which there was now the mechanical means to gratify. The number of readers began to grow, but even in the seventeenth century, the popularity of Sir Thomas Browne (who, remember, was not a Party man in an age of enormous controversy) shows that the standard of the reading public was still high.

Toward the end, however, of the seventeenth century a change occurred. With population and printing the number of readers was also growing. Controversy and persecution had whetted the public appetite for pamphlets and new writers, and the character of prose itself changed. From being a Miltonic and majestic music, copious in quotation and rich (perhaps obese) in Latinisms, it became the vehicle of " questions of the day." The aim of prose became less reflective and more combative : its style more light, its subjects more prosaic, its effects more epigrammatic; and its subject was addressed, less to the scholar in his study than to the wits in their coffee-houses. The public had come upon the scene. With this change English prose assumed its modern character.

With the creation of modern prose, the book and the public (as we now think of them) were begotten, and multiplied through phases on which, being nearer to us, it is needless to insist. But what, exactly, had happened ? Books had been made accessible, reading comparatively common. We must not, I fear, stop there. By making books accessible to the multitude, by converting the general public into a reading public, the multitude had been given access to the instruments, and thus gradually to the centres, of learning. Consider the meaning of this. I ask the reader to neglect, for a moment, the effect of books upon the public, and to concentrate upon the effect of a large reading public upon the quality of literature. Printing does not so much make a present of literature to the multitude as allow the multitude to invade the workshop of letters. Written language, the tool of thought, which was once confined to scholars, its workmen, has been made common property to all who can understand its purport without necessarily understanding its uses or its end.   Just as when a private park is thrown open to the public, flowers and trees are defaced, and litter accumulated, so, when every one is taught to read and given access to literature, letters are misused and defiled.   You cannot make a distinction common property without destroying its distinctiveness.   When Oxford is thrown open to all, all will not become good Oxonians, but Oxford will become indistinguishable from any other place.   All distinctions need protection, for a distinction is, by definition, that which is not common to all.   The indistinct is the undistinguished.   Both accessibility and invasion, then, accrue from the printing of books and the growth of a large reading public.

Since the crowd, by nature " incapable of perfectness," is numerically more powerful than the separate men of genius, and can therefore subdue them more readily than genius can master the crowd, the effect of printing on literature must be, in the long run, more disastrous to literature than it can ever be good for the public.   Even after fifty years of trial, the hopes based on general education still delude many, because people forget that a crowd of schoolchildren is, like any other crowd, always at the same intellectual and moral level.   You cannot make the instruments of education common property without enabling the masses to misuse them to their own hurt. Sincere democrats embrace this point which, however, spits them on it.   Can it be thought that

the newspaper-ridden man of 1925 is more educated than his illiterate country cousin of fifty
years ago ? If he has more information, it is
information less worth having. Nine-tenths of
the information which fills the daily newspapers is
useless, and at least as harmful as the superstitions
of illiterate peasants. We must not applaud the
power to read anything printed in English without
appraising the effect on the reader of that which
he habitually reads. The modern reading public
is duped, hoodwinked, misled, debauched to an
extent which could not be exceeded if it was wholly
ignorant of the alphabet. This is not a partial view
of the facts, nor an outcry against them. It is only
the recognition of the effect of a preceding cause.

You may put it another way. You may say
that the effect of printing on literature has been to
turn an art into an industry, an aid to training into
a branch of commerce. For the crowd is able
richly to reward any writer who appeals to it by
flattering its ignorance or pandering to its
vulgarity. But when the power of the purse
obtains a dominating influence in any of the arts,
the means whereby this power is exercised
becomes the master and not the servant of the art
in question. It may be said that the power of the
purse has always influenced art, but there is all
the difference between the purse of the private
patron, and the purse of the general public. The
private patron is a human being : the general
public is a monster. That is why, despite the

abuses of the private patron, the arts can flourish
under the eye of a despot, and cannot flourish
under that of a demos : they can keep alive
despite it, that is all.   Both despot and demos
control the means of publication.   But the aims of
the patron, even when corrupt, are at least personal and restricted, while the aims of the demos
are anti-personal and pervading.   Americans
constantly tell us that the " tyranny of the
majority, blind, unconscious, and continually
manipulated by rogues or charlatans, grows
always greater " ; and not even Prohibitionists, I
understand, deny that Prohibition was carried in
America by manipulation of the electoral machinery and commercial intrigue, and not by the
mandate of the voters.   The result is that laws in
America are passed without opposition, not
because they are approved, but because respect
for law has been lost, and it has been found that
the only remedy against manipulation of electoral
machinery is to disregard all laws that are dis-
liked.   The familiar cycle from democracy to
anarchy is thus completed.   The crowd is sure to
be something less than human if it is not something more.   When led and disciplined, as in an
army, it may be something more.   When frenzied
and indisciplined as in a mob of voters or of
readers, something less.   The name for something less than humanity is a monster.
    Having glanced at the quality of a large reading
public, and in all crowds humanity is reduced to

its lowest common denominator, let us turn for a moment to the quality of literature, that we may see why it and a monster can never agree with each other. In its origin, all literature was sacred literature. Its subject was divinity, and the ways of divinity were unfolded in Myth and Legend. Now the general definition of a sacred literature or a scripture is a body of writings not fit for every one to read. The subject, being sacred, can be profaned by the uninitiated reader, who himself, even when well-disposed, may suffer hurt from an influence beyond his capacity. One man's meat is poison to a baby : the inconsiderate study of the Bible has driven many persons mad. For this reason, and partly because the primary realities cannot be expressed except in parables, myth and legend are distinguished by possessing double meanings, the one on the surface, the other at the core. But, as civilization altered and languages changed, this initial and interior precaution was found to be insufficient. The further step was taken not only of preserving sacred writings in their original language, but of commenting upon them in the same dead tongue. To both only scholars had access, because it was felt that the mysteries would be profaned if unveiled to all eyes in the vulgar tongue, the tongue, that means, which was the familiar speech of the demos.

In this epoch translations began to make their appearance. But it is interesting to recall that this breach with tradition was not completed without a protest, a protest all the more significant because it was made about one hundred and fifty years after the breach occurred.   The latest spokesman of the traditional view was Dr. Johnson, who hoped, we all remember, and the hope implied a fear, that the walls of Westminster Abbey would never be disgraced by an inscription in English.   (What would have been his reply if some one had asked him whether the stone tables of the Jewish law were incised in the vulgar tongue of Israel ?)   Thus, the quality of literature is, by definition, an unfitness for the mass of readers.   This quality needs always an interior, and generally also an exterior, protection from them.   Because of printing and the reading public, to-day, with the minor exception of poetry, that outer protection to English literature is gone. Poetry is still to a small extent its own protection, because metre is something of a learned tongue. You therefore print things in poetry that you do not print in prose, because the public " makes excuses " for metre, and, as if it were a magistrate, allows " a licence " to the poet that it withholds from the prosaic author !   Patmore published a poem called *Sponsa Dei*.   A prose work on the same subject and with the same title was burnt by him, because a friend said that he was " telling secrets " to the public.   The interesting thing is, that, while the prose was burnt, the poem (note the Latin title) was able to be printed, in English.

The position at which, with the help of a single,

typical instance, we have arrived, is very remarkable. The English demos has brought English
literature to this position. You may now print in
Greek or Latin, French or German, Italian or
Spanish that which you may not print in English.
In New York, to come no nearer home, plays are
allowed in Yiddish that are forbidden in American.
What does this mean ? Either that the English
have a monopoly of decency or that English is the
sole indecent tongue. I leave it to the reader to
decide which is more likely to be true. If the
second alternative is appalling, the first is one by
which our humility is shocked. But, whichever
be true, the effect on our literature is deplorable.
All popular forces are helping to emasculate the
English tongue. Modern English is little more
than the eunuch of its ancient self. A straw which
showed which way the wind is blowing was the
recent *obiter dictum* of a Front Bencher who urged
that the works of Swift and others should no longer
be printed from the original text. The reasons
that he gave were equally applicable to the Authorized Version of the English Bible. Where is all
this to stop ? And who shall decide ? since, if the
process begins at all, no two people will draw the
line at the same place ? But this is by the way.

Any language which refuses to use all its
native resources, which is not free to touch all
subjects, which declines to use the appropriate
word for every thought, has begun to lop off its
limbs. This is the road to suicide. It means, in

sum, that English is ceasing to be the language used by scholars, because they can find (in all completeness) only in foreign tongues the contributions which they need.   Be the subject what you will, from Greek intaglios to psychology, the standard authorities are no longer English ones, not because we have no psychologists or archæologists, but merely because foreign writers freely treat every aspect of their subjects, while their English colleagues can treat, in print, only selected aspects in the mother tongue.   Why ? The reading public has imposed its standard in the holy places of learning.

If you ask, further, why this has not yet happened on the Continent, I do not know.   The fact is certain, but the explanation is doubtful. Something happened to the English at the Reformation (which introduced translations) that did not happen to other Europeans.   The Puritan virus bit us deeply.   An authority suggests to me, in conversation, that the Puritans were more vigorously persecuted abroad, that we only scotched the snake, while they killed it.   Here, anyway, the snake is very much alive, and the English demos is entangled in " frightful nuptials " with it.   Is there any remedy ? or at least alleviation ?   That this may not seem an extravagant question, let us descend from generalizations to familiar facts.

Nowadays the machinery by which books are distributed is even more important than that by which they are manufactured. To print is not to publish. Many printed books are stillborn. For example, the distributing trade took only thirty-six copies of a recent dramatic volume, though the author was well known, at least to connoisseurs. By luck or accident, the papers were dull at the time, and the book had, though latently, a topical appeal. An editor of a big daily saw an opening. The volume was skied on his principal page, and, within three days, the first edition of five hundred copies was exhausted and a new impression required. Now, that which the big newspapers can achieve by such advertisement, the circulating libraries can achieve by pushing books under the noses of their subscribers. It is commonly supposed that subscribers to circulating libraries order the books that they want. But this is the exception. The rule is for them to seek and to accept the advice of assistants in the circulating libraries.[1] Consequently, the books which, capable of popularity at all, succeed, are those which are pushed across the counter. Those which fail, other things being equal, are those which the circulating libraries ignore. Their local managers are also said to be encouraged to put every difficulty in the way of subscribers who apply for books wanted only by a few.

[1] A true story :—

        SUBSCRIBER : Has L. T. Meade written a new book ?
        " TIMES " BOOK CLUB : Not yet, sir.
        SUBSCRIBER : Have you any books like L. T. Meade's ?

Since the distribution of books is as much a business as the distribution of toothpastes and penholders, and the machinery employed is large-scale machinery depending upon and appealing to an enormous number of clients, the circulating libraries do not consider books upon their literary merits, which, of course, are irrelevant to them. They consider, of any book, if it is likely to appeal or not to appeal to the bulk of their subscribers. Since these are timid folk, who wish to follow a lead and have no personal preferences, except for panic, any book of personal literature likely to frighten one subscriber is likely to frighten one hundred thousand of his like. Such a book, naturally, from their point of view, is not accepted by the libraries. It thus must get distributed, if at all, in spite of them. But what of the accepted books ? In the single word of a great artist, the general public is virtually the author of the books which the general public reads. A staple is demanded and supplied by industrious pen-men who have carefully crushed any individuality of their own, because to all crowds a personality, when not appealing to its passions, is distasteful. Like a flower, a personality withers in air breathed by many people. In other words, because the libraries are designed to meet a popular demand, the popular standard of taste is enthroned in the libraries. Our only quarrel with this is on a side, but vital, issue.

Occasionally an author appears who, like Shakespeare, can write a pot-boiler which is also a masterpiece and a masterpiece which is also a pot-boiler. In their several spheres, *As You Like It* and *Esther Waters* are familiar examples. But even the suspicion of that quality which goes to the making of a masterpiece is abhorrent to the general public, because, though we can never define precisely its taste, we can infallibly define its abomination. Its likes, whatever they be, are the opposite of the likes of men and women of letters. The preference of the latter is as distasteful to the public as the preference of the public is irrelevant to the connoisseur. But while the latter will live and let live, *the public is not so charitable*. It has only two attitudes to works of art : applause or persecution. Consequently, even Shakespeare, it appears, occasionally found himself in trouble. Even *Esther Waters*, mighty success as it was, raised an outcry, which is still more familiar to most people than the Esther Waters Home which it inspired. The contemporary man of letters, then, if he is to write freely, has to devise a means to keep the public without. It has invaded his Helicon, and has, or thinks it has, acquired the fee-simple of the sacred hill, by the familiar legal process of squatting there.

The only (proved) solution, for the class of authors which we have in mind, is to publish at a high price for private subscribers. But to do this an author first has to make a reputation. Such a reputation, however, is the result and not the motive of his work ; and when he puts it to the guarding of his freedom, which is also the freedom of literature, he has done as much as a devout disciple can do to check the evil which Caxton's genius unexpectedly set on foot.

In May, 1920, Mr. Hilaire Belloc published an article in *Blackfriars* against " Nationalization." In the course of his argument he said :

" The Capitalists not only own the land and the machinery and the rest of it, they also own the avenues of information. For instance, I could not publish such an essay as this in any one of the great Capitalistic papers or any one of the great Capitalistic reviews. They would not print it. It is the common experience of all those who deal seriously with these problems that they are confined to special organs of opinion which reach but a few."

We have the fact, without the admission, of a censorship. It is the more secure for being unofficial. It has been among the objects of this essay to emphasize the fatality of numbers, and to show that, I will not say a true, but a sincere word, can keep its sincerity only when it disregards a multitudinous appeal. As the bulb grows in the dark underground, so literature germinates beneath the feet and beyond the eye of the general public. In the " special organ of opinion," with tradition at its back, as in the private printing-press, which it resembles, sincerity in literature is most likely to be found.